MORE
FUN
WITH
HOUSE
PLANTS

MORE
FUN
WITH
HOUSE
PLANTS

MARTA BASILA

Brombacher Books • *Richmond, California*

A special thank you goes to Mike Vukelich and M.V. Nurseries, Cayfords' Plant Shoppe, Diablo Nursery, McDonnell Nursery, The Plant Depot, Ferry-Morse Seed Company and Jean Watts for permission to take photographs of their plants.

Mention of a product by trade name in this book is a record of the author's practice and does not constitute a recommendation for its use. It must be emphasized that the proper use of any product requires following the explicit instructions of its manufacturer on the label or package.

Manufactured in the United States of America.
Library of Congress catalog card number: 75-39484
ISBN: 0-89085-079-8

Contents

Foreword

It's no secret that house plants have become a part of our lives. Friends, neighbors, and relatives have them; there is scarcely a home we visit these days that lacks exotic greenery. More recently, the house plant fever has spread to business establishments. We see bank lobbies, doctors' offices, and even auto repair shops handsomely decked out. And it is for good reason—there is nothing as refreshing as the continuous visual pageant provided by living plants.

In response to the ever-growing demand for house plants, there have been books with instructions on their care. Some have been good, and some have not. Most discuss the fifty or sixty varieties most commonly seen in recent years. But what about other common plant species that we can't seem to find any information about? Perhaps the sales person knows the names and general methods of care for these less-talked-about plants, but sometimes you cannot find answers to these common questions. Herein lies the value of this book.

The purpose of this book is decidedly *not* to pay attention to the old favorites. Instead, it goes beyond the scope of books of comparable size in naming and describing, in a well-illustrated encyclopedia, over fifty varieties that for some reason haven't received the attention they deserve. Care has been taken to note the particular foibles of certain plants, necessary remarks as to what kind of environment each plant will thrive in, and a comment or two regarding their original habitats. These references will assist you in creating more natural conditions.

In addition, the book takes into account the necessary items anyone must consider when dealing with any, and all, house plants. How to select a healthy plant, one that's right for you, and how to take care of it once it's in your home are included in several chapters of general discussion. They encompass not only useful but also very interesting information.

The author, Marta Basila, has raised and sold hundreds of varieties—enough to qualify her as an expert on plant care. In addition, she has written a sister volume, *A Book About House Plants*, which has proven very popular.

With your watering can, your pots, and your most valuable tool in hand—this book—you can set forth with confidence to adorn your home or place of business with beautiful house plants.

The Joy of Plants

Plants, plants everywhere!—so beautiful to look at and so satisfying to own! The joy of cultivating house plants has become a common experience these days, and growers are finding out that it really is *easy* to have happy, healthy, plants. You don't need an extensive background in botany or even a whole lot of experience with plants in order for them to thrive in your home, office or school. The basic ingredients for success are some general knowledge about plant care, a little specific knowledge about your particular plant, and a large dose of common sense mixed well therein. (Add a small dash of luck and you certainly have it made.) Experience is a wonderful teacher, so don't stop with one or two plants. Broaden your experience with many more and varied living green (yellow, pink, striped, dotted, etc.) things. The results may prove to be amazingly gratifying!

The more common house plants like philodendron, piggyback, wandering jew and Swedish ivy are very beautiful and fun to grow, but commercial growers are forever coming out with new and unusual plants for you to add to your collection. Some of these plants on the market are truly beautiful, others are grown more for their unusual appearance; all are experiences in themselves and should not be overlooked because they are surely no more difficult to grow than those plants you may already be familiar with.

You may have one or two (or more) failures, but don't become discouraged and give up entirely. Do try to find out what went wrong and use it as a tool to prevent further mistakes. I consider many of my own plants to be rather impressive—but oh! My disasters were certainly impressive too! (They were quickly shuffled into the garbage can before anyone could witness my utter failures.) Don't, however, throw a plant away until it is really dead, dead. Keep trying to correct your mistakes. With determined perseverance a plant may surprise you by reviving and becoming even more astonishingly gorgeous than before. Give it time, care and love. I have found that there are a couple of plants that, as much as I would love to own them, I simply cannot grow for various reasons—one in particular just doesn't like me. But if I had given up when I made those discoveries, I never would have known the joy of growing all sorts of other greenery.

There are certainly many advantages to living plants. They are much more cheering than cut flowers that will soon die; and they are infinitely longer lasting. The real thing is always more gratifying than something artificial; consider living plants instead of plastic ones. Perhaps there is a particular space in your home that you feel needs a piece of furniture or picture. Plants will fill that space beautifully and will be much less expensive than a furniture item. The only disadvantage—and a small one it is—is that plants do require a bit of care. Remember, too, that a well-chosen plant will not only be rewarding, but it will also freshen the air and make your home more attractive. You will also please friends and neighbors by giving

The shrimp plant and tapeworm plant are placed with other house plants for an interesting effect.

them starts from your plants. Think of the satisfaction you'll receive from knowing that your plant needs you and is growing because of your care.

Of course, you can only use house plants in place of interior decorations or furnishings if the particular location you had in mind will fulfill the plant's living requirements. But it does seem worthwhile to find out. Knowing if you can supply the right conditions for a plant, and a little foreknowledge about its care and proper execution of that care, is an almost unbeatable combination. Just rely on your own experience and common sense and remember that neglect is the fastest way to the trash barrel. Keep in mind too that the environment—humidity, light, heat—in individual homes varies, and what may be correct treatment for someone else's plant, may not be good for yours.

Therefore, somebody else's instructions may not be right for your plants. People and books can give you approximate directions, but hardly ever exact ones. Learn to use your index finger to test the soil for moisture. Watch your plant to see if it's happy; if it isn't, it will let you know. Plants have a number of ways to do this, so try to learn to read their trouble signs properly and learn how to correct any problems that might arise. It's really not difficult. I can almost guarantee that your efforts will lead to very satisfying experiences. Plants will make you feel good.

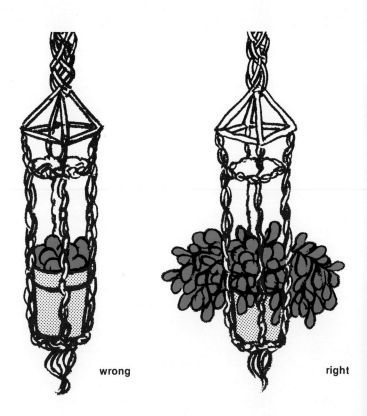

wrong   **right**

The picture on the left shows how not to use a macrame hanger. The plant is so small that it becomes quite insignificant in relation to the elaborate holder. The picture on the right shows how one can be used with plants so that each will emphasize the other's beauty.

1 *So Many to Choose From!*

With so many different plant species and varieties of those species to choose from, it is often very difficult to make a selection. The purchase of a particular plant may seem like an overwhelming decision to make, but you will find your choice narrowed down by the prospective plant's requirements you will be capable of fulfilling. For instance, is it going to be placed in bright or low light? If it is to be low light, you have already eliminated the possibility of those plants that need brighter light. Does it need a lot of water? If it does, will you be able to water often enough? Does it need a lot of humidity? The decision is soon made easier and more likely to be the right one.

Of course the final decision must be made according to your own preference, but you must also consider the plant's needs, if a dead plant was not what you had in mind as a finishing decorative touch. It is quite possible that you and a particular plant are not suited to one another. Your lifestyle may clash with its basic requirements, but there are sure to be some others that will get along quite nicely with you. Perhaps you love dim, cool rooms. A light and warmth-loving plant will certainly not be on its best behavior in such conditions, although it is possible that it will try very hard to tolerate them. Even the hours you keep may affect your plant's well being. If you burn the midnight oil every night, the bright light may confuse a blooming plant that requires a specified number of hours of total darkness in order for its buds to set. On the other hand, if you are an "early to bedder," plants that depend exclusively on artificial light may not be getting enough light to do their best. A busy person may not have time to water a constantly thirsty plant. Someone who works all day may keep the curtains drawn during most of the sunlight hours, depriving the indoor plants of sufficient light. At any rate, it would certainly not be feasible for you to change your lifestyle to conform to your plant's requirements, nor would it be a good idea to purchase a plant that would be miserable because of conditions in which it could not survive. I, myself, have made the mistake a few times of bringing home a plant that was particularly attractive to me, knowing full well that I would probably not be able to give it the care it needed. But more often than not, those "irresistible" plants were soon "resistible" and were written off as failures. Sometimes a plant you're not quite sure will be happy will unexpectedly adapt itself to its new surroundings. But don't push your luck—it can prove discouraging. With so many other plants to choose from, you really don't need to risk disappointments.

Plants do have a considerable margin of flexibility and may survive some rather trying circumstances. Consider the environment of most people's homes compared to the tropics or desert regions which are native to most house plants. Don't be afraid to try to grow one—plants are not at all the mythical fragile things that wither and die at the flick of a black thumb. Instead, plants will do their best to please you.

Plants come in an unbelievable assortment of shapes, sizes, colors and even textures.

For the apprehensive gardener, there are many very hardy varieties of plants to choose from which will not only beautify their allotted space, but also serve to build your confidence. After a few successful experiences you just might get interested enough in plant cultivation to try a more challenging variety.

Keeping in mind the amount of care you are prepared to give a plant, and how challenging a variety you want, your next consideration in choosing a plant should be the degree of light the spot you intend to be the plant's future home receives. This is a very important point. If the space you are thinking of receives a fairly low light, such as a place where light coming through a window is blocked by another building, a tree, or an overhang, there are plants that you should definitely forebear purchasing. If there is enough light for you to cast a shadow on the wall, there are

Where insufficient natural light is available, plants can be made happy with artificial light.

sure to be some plants whose lives will be sustained with a lesser degree of light than they might prefer. But don't choose a flowering plant like the lipstick plant because it will only fade away and die. Most plants with color, other than the usual green in their leaves, need bright light.

On the other hand, you should certainly avoid some plants if the spot you have in mind permits direct sun rays to enter. On a hot summer afternoon few house plants like to sit in a window that faces south or west if it's not shaded by curtains. Remember that window glass magnifies heat and light and extremes of either are not particularly favorable to most house plants. There are exceptions; some house plants enjoy a few hours of direct sunlight. The cactus is the first type that comes to mind. They thrive on light and heat and may even bloom for you if conditions are right.

Proper lighting is one of the most important elements for successful indoor gardening. If there is a particular plant you want, and you think the light level is approximately right, try it. Your plant will soon let you know if it isn't. It should be as easy to remedy an incorrect light situation as it is to tell if the plant is unhappy.

If the light is too strong, thereby burning your plant, yellow and brown glassy patches will appear. A light that is too weak for a plant will cause leaves to fade to a yellow green and eventually fall off. (Yellow leaf drop is also a symptom of improper watering or feeding.) A plant may also indicate that the light is not bright enough by stretching toward the light source or growing new leaves that are consecutively smaller. You can achieve proper lighting by moving your plants closer to, or farther from the window, by shading the window, by adding artificial light, or simply by moving the plant to an area that gets light from another exposure.

A plant-gro light provides the plant-pleasing combination of red and blue light. These lights can usually be purchased at a hardware store, or they can often be ordered through a mail-order catalog. To accomplish the same effect, you can combine fluorescent and incandescent lights yourself. Fluorescent tubes provide light from the blue end of the spectrum, the incandescent bulbs give light from the red. A ratio of two watts fluorescent to one of incandescent is the best practicable combination; more specifically, a 40-watt fluorescent tube and a 20-watt incandescent bulb fulfill this recipe exactly.

If your only source of light is artificial, the light should be left on at least twelve hours a day. One disadvantage of this lighting method will present itself when your electric bill arrives, but the additional charge isn't that great—perhaps a dollar a month will keep your plants happy.

Fluorescent light, used in most office buildings and schools, and incandescent light, which most people have in their homes, will also aid a low-light situation even if used separately. Fluorescent light is preferable to incandescent light, because the filament in incandescent bulbs gives off heat constantly. This heat build-up may harm your plant if the light is on for a long period of time. It not only dries the air around the plant, but there is a chance of the plant becoming burned, so keep plant and incandescent bulb at least 18 inches away from each other.

I wouldn't overly worry about the ideal temperature for a plant, although it is frequently mentioned in plant books. The approximate temperature at which most of us keep our homes is just about right for most plants. In fact, most candidates for house plants are chosen for their adaptability to human living conditions—so unless you keep your house like the arctic or desert regions, don't worry about satisfying most plants' temperature requirements. (By the way, a cactus may love a desert atmosphere, but it is unlikely that you would, and it is certain that you would not want to recreate a tropical rain forest in your living room for the sake of a plant.) Merely put those plants, like stephanotis, that like warmth in the warmer sections of your home if possible, and those that like it cool, like podocarpus, in the cooler areas.

Most house plants prefer a filtered light with a degree of brightness somewhere in between low light and direct sunlight. An eastern exposure, which receives bright light in the morning, is just about perfect for a great majority of plants. North-facing windows provide lower intensity light, but it is constant and more even than light from the other exposures. West and south-facing windows allow a bright light to enter, but they have the disadvantage of often becoming too warm to make plants perfectly happy. A western exposure particularly, frequently requires

Different plants prefer
different light exposures.
Sedum enjoys the
bright light of a south-facing
window.

shading on summer afternoons. Of course, light intensity
does vary in a room according to how close an area is to a
window. The middle of a large room will not receive nearly
as much light as a windowsill does. Remember, too, that
the degree of light also depends on a number of factors
such as reflection from a concrete patio, or shading from a
tree. For further help, see the light requirements chart on
the inside of the back cover.

You will want to choose the healthiest plant possible
to bring home. The better the condition a plant is in, the
better it will look, and the better it will grow. The transi-
tion from shop to home should be an easy adjustment for a
healthy plant to make. Here are some checking points to
take heed of when purchasing greenery:

1. What condition is the foliage in? Are there yellow
leaves which indicate improper watering? Brown leaf
edges may mean not enough water or humidity, too much
heat, or too much fertilizer. (However, some plants, most

notably dracaenas and maranta, seem to develop brown leaf edges even when they are in perfect health.) Holes or spotted discoloration may mean the presence of pests. If the leaves are faded looking, possibly the plant has not received enough light.

2. Does the plant look wilted? It may be on sale for that very reason, so beware—a damaged plant very often will not prove to be the bargain you hoped.

3. Plants whose leaves grow along a single stem, like ivies, should have evenly spaced leaves that are not too far apart. If it is leggy, it is not only less attractive, but it may indicate that it was forced into fast foliage growth in the greenhouse and that the root system may not have had enough time to develop properly.

4. Roots growing out of the pot are a pretty sure indication that repotting will be necessary right away. Don't buy it unless you don't mind the extra fuss.

5. If you are considering a flowering plant, is it blooming out of season? This indicates that it has been forced in a hot house and it will soon complete its flowering cycle and generally not bloom again until the following year. If you buy this one, just don't expect it to bloom at the proper season.

If you have chosen a plant that seems to be healthy, it will most surely thrive in its new home and bring you immense pleasure.

2 From the Store to Your Door

It is seldom that much thought is given to the transportation of a plant from the store to its prospective home. It is, however, something that you should be concerned about. The beautiful healthy plant you just purchased can lose much of its glossy good health in one quick trip if the proper precautions are not taken. Bruising, breaking or shocking the plant will make its initial adjustment to new surroundings a lot more difficult, besides decreasing its beauty.

If it happens to be one of the colder months, remember that your plant has most recently become accustomed to the warmth of a heated store, and carrying it outside unprotected is likely to induce shock. Such sudden changes in temperature will cause leaves to drop, sometimes a few days later. Once this starts many leaves may follow very suddenly, so you could end up with nothing but a stalk or stem. Ask for some paper to wrap around the plant, or for a large paper bag to slip plant and pot into. Be careful of stems and leaves when you wrap your plant; get the paper around them so they aren't bent into positions where they'll break off if pressure is applied.

If the plant is riding home in a car, don't place it directly in front of the heater which will dry it out and burn it. Don't do the opposite though, and leave it in an un-heated car for any lengthy period of time or it will freeze.

The mistake of leaving plants in a hot, airless car on a very warm day is more frequently made. You wouldn't do that to your dog; don't do it to your plant—it needs air to breathe as much as any other living thing, so don't suffo-cate it. Even if the car windows are kept open to let in air, the heat under the car roof and sunlight coming directly into the car could be quite harmful. Plants will lose mois-ture and shrivel in no time. Remember, too, that just as you shouldn't put your plants in front of the heating vent, the same holds true for its opposite, the air conditioner.

Once in the car the best and easiest way to handle the plant is simply to have a willing friend hold it for you. However, if you made this shopping trip alone, you will have to settle for second best and place it on the car seat or the floor of the car, being careful not to damage any of the leaves or fronds. If you have a trailing variety, drape the leaves carefully. To avoid damage to the leaves, put the plant into a large paper bag or make a paper collar around it, using the pot to shape it, so that the trailing leaves go up, not out and down, and are protected by the paper.

Be careful to balance the pot properly when you set it down, otherwise a sudden stop may cause it to plummet. Prop it with anything handy to prevent it from falling against, or off, the seat. These precautions may take a little extra time, but the effort is certainly worth it to as-sure that the perfect plant you picked out gets home in that same condition.

3 Make Your Plant Feel at Home

Now that you have purchased a plant, do your best to help it make a smooth and easy adjustment to its new environment. The first welcome a foliage plant (but not a succulent) should receive is a process called leaching. Leaching is the passing through of a liquid—in this case, tepid water—to carry off soluble components. What you are doing is helping rid the soil of any excess salts and fertilizers that may be in it. So carry your plant to a sink or bathtub and give it a thorough watering. Add water at the top of the pot until it runs out through the drainage holes at the bottom. When the water stops running out of the pot, do it again. Repeat this process four times—adding water until it runs out, then watering again. Perhaps I should add that if the pot your plant is in has no drainage holes, this method is obviously not going to work. You will only waterlog the plant. So do check to make sure that the water has a way out of the pot.

Have a little care with the water you use on plants. Always use water that is at room temperature or just slightly warmer. Cold water shocks a plant's root system and hot water cooks the roots. Either one will certainly not benefit your plant and may do considerable damage. Be careful of spattering foliage with water. Cold water will leave unsightly markings on some delicate-leaved plants, and the opposite, hot water, will burn foliage.

Never, under any circumstances, use water that has been run through a water softening system. The chemicals used in such systems bode no good for your plants—it is very possible that such chemicals will burn them. Instead, resort to water from your outdoor tap, or rain water.

Don't water directly onto the crown of a plant because repeated waterings of this sort may easily rot out the plant's center. Try to direct your stream of water under the foliage, directly into the soil in the pot. More importantly, never water blindly, that is, without first checking the moisture content of the plant's soil at least by sight, or more preferably, by touch. I cannot stress enough how easy it is to kill a plant by lovingly overwatering it. Try awfully hard to avoid making this mistake—but don't be so apprehensive about watering that you neglect your plants altogether. Strike a happy medium and all should be well.

Not always a necessity, but frequently beneficial to house plants, is the addition of moisture to the air around your plants. Most house plants originated in a tropical environment, and the dry atmosphere of your home does not exactly duplicate their native lands. Although they will generally tolerate the drier conditions, they would certainly appreciate and probably grow better with humid air around them. This can be achieved in a number of ways. A bottle with a spray nozzle attached to it, called a "mister," can be utilized to project a fine spray of water over the plants. (This also helps rid the leaves of dust and helps prevent the attack of those pests that are attracted to dry, dusty places.) Most ferns, and other moisture-loving plants, would love to be misted once or even twice a day if you have the time. However, hairy-leaved plants, like the hanging velvet vine, don't care for a spray showered upon

Many plants appreciate the extra humidity they receive from a dry well set-up.

them because it traps dust in the fine hairs of their foliage. A coleus will quickly show its disapproval of misting by fading the color from its leaves. Other methods of adding moisture to the air which may be used in addition to misting or by themselves, are creating dry wells for your plants or simply placing saucers of water around your plants. A dry well can be made by filling a saucer with pebbles, and resting the plant's pot in the pebbles. Then water can be added to the saucer until the level reaches just below the bottom of the pot. You don't want the pot to sit in water, which will clog the drainage holes, but rather to let the water evaporate around the plant adding moisture to the air. Another, more expensive but very effective method of increasing the humidity, is to purchase a humidifier. Although it will certainly cost a bit, a humidifier should benefit your health along with your plants'.

Don't feed your plant for a month or more after you bring it home. A stimulus like fertilizer will only divert its energies from adjusting to its new surroundings, and it needs time to do just that. Another good reason for withholding food at this time is because the plant may have been recently fed at the nursery, and although you leached out the soil, a residue may be left. So don't risk burning or shocking your plant with an immediate feeding.

By the same token, don't repot it right away. Let it accustom itself to its new environment before you disturb its roots. Wait at least two weeks before repotting a newly purchased plant.

You might, however, give your plant some Vitamin B-1 or "Superthrive" to absorb shock and stimulate its roots toward vigorous growth.

If, after a few days, you notice lower leaves turning yellow and dropping off, check to make sure that your plant is receiving enough light and that you are not over-watering it. If you think everything seems all right on those counts, the yellow leaves are probably only the plant's reaction to finding itself in new growing conditions. Just snip the leaves off, or wait for them to fall, and then remove them from the soil surface. Dead material in the pot may decay and harbor pests or diseases. If many leaves continue to drop and it seems as though you are going to be left with only a stem, it is likely that the plant's root system was not developed enough for it to withstand the change. This instance does not happen often, as most reliable greenhouses are careful, but sometimes a plant is forced into rapid foliage growth to reach a marketable size quickly, thereby depriving the roots of time to develop properly. So although this occurence is rare, if you do find it happening, take your plant back and question the dealer. Keep in mind though, that harsh mishandling on your part between the store and your home, or soon there-after, may also have caused the plant to go into severe shock.

4 Give Your Plant Proper Care

Along with the proper amount of light, the correct amount of water is extremely important for plant survival—as with light, too much or too little can be disastrous. First find out approximately what kind of watering care a particular plant requires—does it like evenly moist soil, or soil that is left to dry out slightly or a lot between waterings? Then determine for yourself what watering habits best suit your plant by observing it carefully for a few weeks. The best way to tell how much moisture the soil is holding is to insert your index finger up to the first joint into it. If the soil is dry and crumbly, or so dry and hard packed that your finger won't even dent it, you should probably water (unless it is a succulent). If the soil sticks to your finger and is dark colored, it's undoubtedly moist; if the soil feels wet, not damp, and water wells up into the depression left by your finger, the plant is almost certainly overwatered.

If you think it likely that the soil is waterlogged, check your drainage holes to be sure they are not plugged. Gently and carefully insert a pencil through them so that the dirt that may be stopping a free flow is disturbed. But don't push so hard that roots are broken or the piece of crock shard that should be at the bottom of the pot is shoved up into or through the root mass.

Finger test for soil moisture. Index finger should penetrate to first joint and come out with moist, but not wet, soil sticking to it.

Overwatering is very easy to do, especially since wilted foliage is a sign of both too much water and not enough. It is so simple to just pour on more water without checking the soil first, thereby giving your plant a fatal dose. Be faithful about actually feeling the soil before giving your plants a drink so that you avoid this kind of trouble.

Never continue a set watering schedule for a plant without checking to see if it is reacting favorably. Remember that changing factors such as heat, wind, and humidity can make a considerable difference as to the water intake of a plant. A plant hanging in front of a window that is left open during the summer to allow a warm breeze will dry out a lot faster than it did in the colder months when the window was kept closed. For the same reason, don't ever follow to the letter someone else's specific directions for watering. If a nurseryman, for instance, tells you to water three times a week, keep in mind that it is only a guideline to follow. You are the only one that can determine what your plant needs. The environment in your home varies from someone else's home, just as it varies throughout the year. Remember, too, that the frequency of watering depends upon what size and kind of pot your plant is in. Although your neighbor may water her fern twice a week, and the atmosphere in her home is similar to yours, you are almost certainly going to need to water yours more often if hers is in a plastic pot and yours is in an unglazed clay pot. Water evaporates more quickly from terra cotta pots than from plastic or glazed ones. A plant in a small pot will dry out more rapidly than one in a larger pot. The air circulation around hanging plants dries them out more rapidly than one in a standing pot. Always remember that plants need more water in their growing season than during the time that they are resting or possibly completely dormant. General rules for watering:

Always use tepid water, never hot or cold water that will shock the plant.

Morning is the best time to water, mist, or feed plants. As the sun heats the atmosphere, the water warms and evaporates. The afternoon sun may heat the water up enough to do root damage, and the cooling evening air may invite fungus diseases.

Always water thoroughly rather than just a little at a time. A sparse watering only dampens the soil surface and evaporates faster than the plant can assimilate it, causing water stress in the plant.

Never use water that has been run through a water softening system.

Never water directly onto the crown of a plant.

Never leave your plant in a saucer full of water longer than 30 minutes. The plant cannot receive oxygen from the bottom and subsequently, the roots will rot.

Plants receive a thorough watering when their pots are immersed in a pail of water. Plants with shrunken root balls benefit greatly from this practice.

Sometimes, a plant seems to be wilted and dry all the time, even if you water it frequently. If the water runs out of the pot as fast as you are pouring it in, chances are the root ball has shrunken away from the sides of the pot and the water is running out between the soil and root mass and the pot. Try correcting this by immersing plant and pot in a pail of tepid water until the water level is just over the rim of the pot. Wait until the bubbling stops and then take the pot out of the pail and let it drain. The bubbling is caused by water filling the air pockets in the soil and forcing the air out. This is also a good method to use to water all of your plants thoroughly, but don't do it more than once a week. If this treatment hasn't loosened a particular stubborn root ball, you'll have to lift plant and all out of the pot, gently massage most of the soil away from the roots, and put the plant back in the same pot with new moist soil all around it.

Knocking out. A sharp rap loosens soil and plant, and the whole potful slides out into protecting hand.

It may also be that your plant isn't taking any water because its roots have outgrown its pot. The most obvious indication of this condition is roots growing out of the pot's drainage hole. Sometimes, though, small roots find their way out of the pot's holes even when there is plenty of space for them to grow in the soil. The best way to make sure your plant really needs a new home is to lift it out of its pot and check the soil ball. If you see more roots than soil, it's time to repot. The simple method of taking your plant out of its pot is called "knocking out." Just turn plant and pot upside down, supporting the plant with a hand spread around the stem and over the soil, and rap the pot sharply against a solid surface to loosen the root ball. With a gentle pull, the plant should slide out with the root ball intact. However, a stubborn plant may require some assistance. If the pot is not of any value, break it away from the plant with a few sharp cracks, or loosen the soil around the

edges of the pot with the aid of a spoon. Then gently pry it out trying to disturb the roots as little as possible.

Now that you are sure that your plant needs a new home—and if you had the above-mentioned trouble getting it out of its pot, it almost certainly does want a new home—be sure to choose the correct size pot. Never transplant into a pot that is more than 2 inches larger in diameter than the plant's old home. Your basic purpose in repotting is either to make the plant look prettier in a decorative container, or simply to aid its growth. A small plant in a large pot will not only look lost, but it may have a serious growth setback and possibly even die. It will make every effort to fill up the extra space and touch the pot sides with its roots, sacrificing foliage growth to devote more energy to its roots. Sometimes the foliage is so severely sacrificed that it dies back completely. House plants like to be a little crowded; they don't like a lot of extra root space. Transplant into a pot only one size larger, and only if necessary.

Of course, you needn't repot your plant in another "pot"—you can utilize any number of waterproof containers providing you clean them thoroughly first. Try using a teacup or mug, a plastic lined basket, an ice bucket, a copper teapot, or even an interesting old jar instead of terra cotta, plastic or glazed pots. It is preferable to choose a container that has good drainage, but it certainly isn't always possible. If you have chosen one that you cannot make a drainage hole in, one of two remedies is possible. One choice is to place a pot, which does provide for good drainage, on a layer of pebbles inside the preferred, pretty container. The other alternative is to place in the bottom of the pot a layer of crock shards or pebbles for drainage, then a layer of charcoal to filter the water and keep it sweet, followed by a layer of soil so that you can transplant directly into the pot.

If you have chosen a conventional pot but can't decide between plastic or clay, there are some points to consider about each. A plant in a clay pot can breathe better, and the pot is fairly heavy and therefore cannot be tipped over as easily as its lighter counterpart. On the other

Two methods of utilizing a decorative container without drainage holes are illustrated. The plant and its pot may be placed in the container, or planted directly into the container.

Root ball is so crowded that water cannot be absorbed into the soil in order for the plant to utilize it. Water will run straight through such a mass.

hand, water evaporates more rapidly and a plant in a clay pot will have to be watered more often than one in plastic.

A clay pot will also break if it is dropped. Plastic pots have long been disparaged because they haven't the porous nature of the terra cotta. However, I find that plastic makes a better hanging pot because it is far lighter than clay. Because it also holds moisture better, I prefer it to clay for plants that must never be allowed to dry out. Plastic has the additional advantages of being less expensive, coming in a variety of colors, and being relatively unbreakable.

Always clean any pot you choose to use, but if you're using a pot that has previously contained a plant, be especially sure to scrub all of the old soil away from the sides of the pot with a stiff brush and warm soapy (biodegradable) water. Rinse all the soap out afterward.

Terra cotta pots should be soaked in water before you plant in them. The reason is that a more or less dry pot will absorb a considerable amount of moisture and, when you water a freshly potted plant, you want to be sure the water reaches the plant and doesn't soak into the pot and evaporate from its surface.

Next, if you're using a pot that has a large drainage hole through which the soil might fall or wash out, put some pieces of crocking (old clay potshards—break up a small pot if necessary), convex side up, in the bottom of the pot, or a layer of pebbles. You want to prevent the soil from washing out, but water must still be allowed to flow through. Never use pebbles that have been collected at the beach because salt from sea water would be very harmful to your plant. Now fill the pot halfway with soil. Always use moist soil when potting; dry soil does not readily absorb water and the plant's roots may be damaged.

There are a number of good commercial potting soils on the market. They contain all of the components that will satisfy most plants—usually one part soil, one part sand, perlite, or some other sharp material for good drainage, and one part organic material like peat moss to hold moisture.

Other than the fact that using a packaged soil is more convenient than mixing your own, the risk of the soil harboring pests or diseases is limited because the soil has been sterilized. You might be amazed at the potential harm that can be carried in on a trowel full of garden soil. Of course, you can sterilize your own soil by baking it in an oven set at 250° for about an hour, but it's a messy, smelly business, besides being time consuming. However, if you really prefer making your own soil mix, use equal parts of sterilized garden soil, builders' sand, perlite, etc. or ver-

Components of a good potting soil, which is shown in center. From the top, reading clockwise: sand, leaf mold, fir shavings, perlite, peat moss.

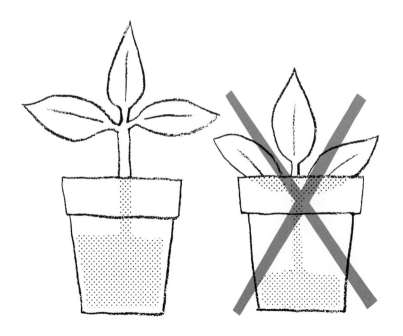

Fill the pot with enough soil so that the plant will be at the correct height in the pot.

miculite, and peat moss. After it is well mixed, dampen it thoroughly and it is ready to use.

Cacti and other succulents require a slightly different growing medium. They prefer an equal mixture of sand and potting soil. Don't use ocean sand for the same reason you shouldn't use pebbles collected at the shore; the salts may harm the plant. (It also tends to pack down instead of acting as drainage material.) For more information on mixing a growing medium for succulents refer to chapter 11 . If you prefer not to make your own, it is possible to buy a cactus mix at most nurseries.

You will want your plant to adjust to its new pot as rapidly as possible. To send the roots in the right direction, gently massage the root ball to loosen up tangled roots. Sometimes if this is not done when the roots are very tightly entangled, they will never stretch out into the new soil, but will remain in a root mass of the original pot's shape, growing tighter and tighter until they strangle themselves. In such a case, the needed nutrients in the new soil are never assimilated and the plant will starve or die of thirst, so do loosen up the roots without tearing them.

Place the plant on its roots in your half-filled pot. Put in or take out some soil if it appears that the height of the plant won't be right. The final soil level should be about one-half inch below the rim of the pot so that you can water the plant easily. When you're satisfied that the plant is at the right height, add some more potting mix and gently tamp it down around the roots, working inward from the edges of the pot. Never fill the pot to the top. If the soil fills up the entire pot, the water will run off and over the edges before it has time to soak in.

At this point, water the plant thoroughly to rid the soil of air pockets. You might choose to add some Vitamin B-1 to the water to help minimize transplant shock. An-

Fish Emulsion
Fertilizer 5-2-2

A.   B.   C.

NON-BURNING • 100% FISH, DEODORIZED

The numbers that often appear on plant food labels indicate the proportion of ingredients in the complex. In this typical house plant food, (a.) 5 stands for Nitrogen, a leaf growth stimulator; (b.) 2 represents Phosphorus, for root hardiness; and (c.) 2 indicates potash, which aids assimilation of the nutrients by the plant.

other product I believe in is called "Superthrive." It is a vitamin and hormone supplement that can be used in addition to your plant food. Both products are great for sick and healthy plants alike. Just be sure to read the directions carefully and don't overdo it.

After watering and draining your plant, give the pot a thump on a solid surface to further settle the soil. Now put it back in its place. Don't feed a newly potted plant for a couple of weeks. Give it time to adjust to its new home. Feeding is a very important part of plant care though, and should not be neglected. Your plant will run out of nutrients in the soil in which it is potted after awhile, so they should periodically be replenished to prevent starvation. No matter what type of fertilizer you use, and they do come in many forms—liquids, powders, tablets and time-released capsules—be very sure to read the directions carefully. A little less than the recommended dosage is better than too much, but try to follow the directions as accurately as possible. Some plant foods require that you use them in pre-moistened soil which means you should water your plants a few hours ahead of feeding them.

Any house plant food you get should have three numbers on its label, like 5-1-1 or 4-10-10. This number code tells you the ratio in which the most important elements are contained in your fertilizer. These elements are, respectively, nitrogen (N), phosphorus (P), and potassium (K), the latter usually in the form of potash.

Nitrogen is the most quickly taken in by the plant. It stimulates foliage growth and gives the plant a rich green color. Phosphorus encourages flower development, aids the stems in hardening, and helps the roots grow. Potassium also helps the roots and stems to mature and flower buds to develop. Perhaps even more important, phosphorus aids in building a sturdy plant that can more easily cope with temperature extremes and will be more disease resistant.

In general terms, if it's a foliage plant you want to feed, give it a fertilizer whose first number is highest, because you want more nitrogen for a lush green plant. If it's a flowering plant, like a lipstick, give it a fertilizer whose second number is as high or higher than the first, because you want to encourage flower development with phosphorus, not a lot of leaf growth. Cacti should also be fed with a fertilizer low in nitrogen.

Never feed a sick plant, and don't feed a dormant plant. The dormancy period of a plant is its rest period. You'll know this is occurring when the plant slows down its growth or stops altogether for no apparent reason. This usually happens in the winter, so hold off the food for a couple of months. In fact, it's good to give plants a break from feeding even if they're not dormant. You might stop feeding them through December and January, picking up with a slowly increasing feeding schedule again in February.

It really is rather important to stick to some kind of feeding schedule. A consistent schedule is easier on the plants and they will show even growth, plus you won't run the risk of feeding too soon after having already done so. If you have neglected to fertilize your plant for awhile, don't try to make up for lost time by giving it an extra large dose. Too much fertilizer will burn the plant's roots down to stubs, so don't think that if a little is good, more is better. You'll be inviting disaster.

You might find it a good idea to keep a record of your feeding schedule on a calendar to be doubly certain of when you last fed a plant.

Most plants like a lot of humidity and will appreciate being misted as frequently as possible. It not only adds moisture to the air, but helps to keep them clean too. You might also bathe your plants occasionally to keep them dust free. The foliage of your small plants can be swished around in water and a biodegradable soap. Just turn them upside down and hold the dirt in by spreading your fingers around the plant's stem, palming the soil surface. After bathing them, rinse them off in tepid water. Your larger plants can be sponge bathed with the soapy water and then rinsed the same way, or with the garden hose. Just be gentle with the hose so that you don't flatten the plant with a strong stream of water. When you do wash your plants, be sure to do the undersides of the leaves where pests may be hiding. Don't use cell-clogging plant leaf polishes; these only attract more dust in the long run.

Groom your plants periodically by snipping off brown leaf edges, dead leaves, or broken parts with sharp scissors. If any vegetation has fallen to the surface of the soil, clean it off—fungus diseases and pests just love decaying vegetation. Don't cut off those long runners your fern puts out unless they have turned brown and died. They help aerate the soil and are the plant's means of propagation. Tuck them back into the soil of the pot and they may form baby ferns on the tips.

SOAPY WATER

RINSE WATER

Small plants can be swished in soapy water—not detergent—and then rinsed off with clear water.

Plants reach toward the light, so if you have a plant facing a bright window on one side and a darker room on the other, remember to turn it occasionally so that all sides of the plant get equal time with the light. If you don't, you may end up with a lopsided plant instead of an evenly rounded one. Don't, however, move a plant that is getting ready to bloom. They become very touchy at this stage and may drop their blossoms if they are moved.

Another way to control the shape of your plant is to prune or pinch it. This not only shapes the plant, but promotes more vigorous growth. Those plants for which

**Rotate plants frequently
to avoid lopsided growth
towards the light source.**

pruning or pinching is recommended (refer to the encyclo-pedia section of this book) should definitely receive the treatment. I find that many people are afraid to cut off any healthy growth because they think that since the plant is growing, it must be doing well, and interference may harm it. I cannot stress enough that pruning or pinching is beneficial for plants and they will soon have an improved appearance. Think of it not so much as cutting something off, but as adding growth to the plant; one tip removed may force many more leaves or stems to grow. Pinching is done to soft-stemmed plants like the coleus or tiger plant. If you pinch out the new tip growth, more lateral buds will form along the stem, giving your plant a more bushy appearance. If you neglect this treatment, you could easily

42

end up with a very leggy, unattractive plant. Prune the harder-stemmed plants with a sharp knife or pruning shears. Plants like the lipstick and columnea should be pruned not only for shape, but also to encourage flower development. In late winter or early spring, before new growth starts, they should be pruned back severely—I know, it took so long for it to grow you can't bear to hack it off—but do so or you may have an unattractive, non-blooming plant next year. Just remember that they will reward you with vigorous, fresh growth, and that most flowering plants produce blossoms only on new shoots—the more new growth, the more flowers you will have. Fast growing plants, like the wandering jew, can rapidly get out of hand if they are not carefully controlled. They will shed more leaves if they are left to grow longer and longer with no shaping. Please don't be afraid to cut—your plant may temporarily look poorly, but it will soon show you how much it appreciates your care by becoming more beautiful than you had hoped.

Fresh air is good for your plants, but be careful about setting them directly in front of open windows or doors except on mild days. The sudden blasts of air not only evaporate the moisture from the air around and on the

Pinching out the growing tip to make a plant grow lateral leaves and fill out to bushier form.

43

plant, but the difference in temperature from the air outside and that in your home may shock the plant, and its dropped leaves will tell you how it feels. "Listen" to it or you may end up with just a stem. Placing a plant in front of a door that is used frequently or in the direct path of the air-conditioning or heating vent is perhaps even more harmful.

Be wary of cooking your plants' roots by setting them on a radiator, a television or anything else that emits heat. In cold weather protect plants that sit next to a window by placing sheets of cardboard between them and the glass at night—or simply by moving them to another location. The temperature really drops by a glass window and your plant may freeze if precautions are not taken.

You may choose to summer some of your house plants outside. House plants can often provide lush greenery in shady places where many "outdoor" plants won't do well. Don't, for heaven's sake, place them in direct sun or they will be dead in no time. Also keep in mind that the depth of shade outdoors is often entirely different than that of shade indoors. Be sure your plants are in a protected area, like upon a porch, on a covered patio, or beneath a tree's branches, and give them extra water if they seem to require it. They probably will, because of the breezes and heat that they are not accustomed to from indoor living. It is good practice to start them outside for only a few hours in the morning the first day and to add another hour or so every day until they have adjusted to a full day outside. A sudden change of environment may shock the plant so it is a good idea to do the same when you bring the plants in again before cold weather arrives. When you do bring them indoors again, check carefully for pests and diseases and clean them thoroughly so that nothing harmful is transmitted to your other plants. By taking a few precautions, you shouldn't have any trouble with your plants.

5 Pests and Other Problems

We all know the old adage "an ounce of prevention is worth a pound of cure," and it applies very well in the case of house plant ailments. That shaky little stem with a mere two leaves on it which was once a lush plant, will take much time and care to recover its former beauty. Quite possibly such a failure could have been avoided. It is important to be sure that the plant you purchase is as healthy as possible to begin with. When any plant or cut flowers are brought into the house, be certain that they are free of pests or diseases. Trouble spreads rapidly to other plants. Use only sterilized potting soil to avoid spreading bugs and bacteria. Keep your plants dust and soil free. The leaves of most foilage plants can be wiped by a damp sponge or sprayed with lukewarm water. A small camel's hair brush can be used to clean fuzzy-leaved plants like the African violet. Keep your plants well groomed by removing all dead, withered or infected vegetation. Always wash your hands after handling an infected plant. Keep an eye on a newly purchased plant or one that has been moved to a different location to see if it is adjusting happily. Try to check all of your plants periodically, looking under the leaves and at the leaf joints for possible trespassers and intruders. Early symptoms of pest invasion frequently go undetected until the plant is well on its way to the grave. Do your best to discover what type of care each plant needs and carry it out.

Cleanliness and proper care are the key factors involved in problem prevention, but sometimes, in spite of good intentions and loving care, trouble strikes. If you are fairly certain that you are doing what would normally keep your plant healthy, it may be that it is infested with one or

Fuzzy-leaved plants can be kept dust-free by brushing their foliage with a camel hair brush.

another of the pests common to house plants. Immediately isolate the plant so that the invaders, if any, won't spread to other plants in your collection. Then try to determine which particular attacker has besieged your plant and proceed to take the proper measures. Never for any reason feed a failing plant; however, a dose of Vitamin B-1 might help it on its way to recovery. Since plants ingest (take in) food through their leaves as well as their roots, you might also try putting a drop or two of Vitamin B-1 in your misting device when you spray. Don't do this more often than every two weeks. You needn't limit this Vitamin B-1 shower to ailing plants; healthy plants will also benefit from an occasional misting with Vitamin B-1.

If your plant is only slightly infested, it is always best to try to wash off the pests with soapy (biodegradable) water, rather than resort to a pesticide. Sponge off a large plant with the soapy water, especially the undersides of the leaves, and then rinse it off with a garden hose. The soapy water, incidentally, will not harm the plant if it soaks into the soil in the pot. Just make sure you've used biodegradable soap; the chemicals will break down into elements the plant can use or that will leach out in your regular soil washing. If it's a small plant you're disinfesting, you can turn it upside down (supporting the stem and soil with one hand, getting the plant's main stem between a couple of your fingers), and swish it around in a sink full of lukewarm soapy water. Then rinse it off with tepid water from the tap.

However, if you decide to use an insecticide of any kind, be sure to read the directions on the container carefully. Not only can the chemicals harm your plant if used improperly, but you as well. *Carry your plants outdoors to spray them*—if used in a closed space, pesticides can make you, and every other living thing in the area, quite ill. Never use chemical sprays on a windy day or while you

Enlarged illustrations of white fly and aphid.

are eating or smoking. Don't mix up more than you can use at one time; but if there is some left over, get rid of it carefully. Always wash your hands and face thoroughly after working with a pesticide and store it cautiously. If you are using a pesticide in an aerosol can, be sure to spray the plant from twelve to eighteen inches away. Freon, the chemical that keeps the spray pressurized, will burn your plant if you get too close with your spray. After using any insecticide, rinse the plant off with clear water when the solution has dried.

If you've given up all hope for a house plant that is badly infested, throw plant, pot, and soil away. Don't re-use the pot or soil as they may harbor eggs or larvae that might not be destroyed by a simple washing.

Aphids

Aphids are plant lice that feed by sucking the plant juices, causing new growth to stunt and foliage to pale and curl. They are tiny green, black, or red soft-bodied insects that can usually be found along new growth tips and the undersides of leaves, especially along the veins. Aphids frequently ride in unannounced on cut flowers or plants brought in from out of doors. Of the house plants, the purple violet is one of their favorite meals. Pick or wash off aphids if they are few in number. For a heavily infested plant, use products containing a systemic or malathion.

48

Enlarged illustrations of mealy bug and scale.

Mealybug

This pest looks like a tiny bit of fuzzy white cotton or furry mold. Mealybugs suck the plant sap, stunting and eventually killing the plant. You'll find them congregated along stems and undersides of leaves, very often in the joint where a stem branches or a leaf grows out. They are particularly fond of crotons and coleuses. For very mild cases apply a Q-tip dipped into rubbing alcohol to the bugs and then wash them off. You might have to go over the plant several days in a row, as the mealybug is particularly persistent. If this method does not control the infestation, or if your plant is heavily populated, spray with malathion and repeat the treatment one week later. An alternate method of control would be the use of a systemic pesticide for house plants. This method eliminates a second spraying because the systemic is taken up into the plant itself. Keep a careful watch on any plant that has had mealybugs once, because they do reappear.

Red Spider Mite

The spider mite is invisible to the naked eye, so the first signs of its presence you'll see are mottled yellow and brown speckles on the foliage, or a fine webbing under leaves and at leaf joints. Mites love ivies and piggybacks and scheffleras. They thrive in hot dry air, so misting and placing susceptible plants in cooler locations of your

49

house might help prevent or minimize an attack. If your plant has red spider mite, isolate it immediately; the bug spreads rapidly. Spray with malathion or a systemic, or some other pesticide whose label indicates mite control.

Scale

Another pest that sucks vital plant juices is the scale insect. Scale usually appears as a hard, oval, brown bump, although it can also be white or black. The actual bug is inside the hard case it has made for itself. (Just as an aside, lacquer is often made from the hard growth covering an East Indian scale insect; that will give you some idea of the protection these insects provide for themselves.) They show up on the undersides of leaves along the main veins. Ferns are particularly susceptible, but don't confuse the brown spore cases of the fern with scale. Spore cases are most often irregularly spaced and spread out on the undersides of leaves, whereas scale is usually lined up exactly along the main veins where the insect has access to the plant's juices. If there are only a few scales, try picking them off with your fingernails. Otherwise, spray with malathion or a systemic pesticide.

White fly

White fly is a difficult invader to banish from your plant. The adult fly can usually be seen on the undersides of leaves, however it is their larvae that do the real damage by sucking plant juices. A systemic pesticide should be used so that you are sure to destroy the entire cycle of eggs, larvae, and flies.

If it doesn't seem to be a pest that is causing your plant to decline, check its symptoms further. '

Leaf drop

Lower leaves that turn yellow and drop off could be attributed to a number of causes.

What's this plant's problem?

This hypothetical plant is besieged by a number of ills which could have been prevented with a little bit of care.

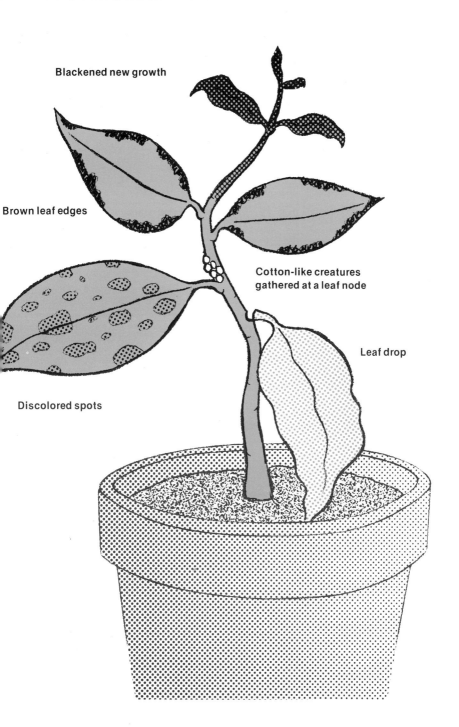

Blackened new growth

Brown leaf edges

Cotton-like creatures gathered at a leaf node

Leaf drop

Discolored spots

Using pencil to keep drainage hole i
pot open. Gentle push is needed to
keep from moving crock shard or
injuring roots.

If your plant has just recently been added to your collection or brought into your house from out-of-doors, it might only be going through a period of adjustment. Is your plant sitting in a draft? Sudden changes in temperature and drafts cause leaf drop.

More often, yellow leaves mean overwatering. Too much water given too often keeps the air spaces in the soil filled so that the roots of the plant are not able to get needed oxygen. Check the saucer under your plant to see if it's full of water. Check to see if the pot's drainage hole is clogged by carefully inserting a pencil to loosen the soil. If water level and drainage hole check out, you are simply watering too frequently. Let the plant dry out until it wilts *slightly*, and then start a new water cycle.

If the soil is really soggy, you might lift your plant out of its pot to check the roots. If the soil and roots smell very sour (you'll know it if it does!), your plant's roots are rotting and there's not much hope of saving the plant. However, if you want to make a final valiant effort, gently remove most of the soil from around the roots and remove the damaged sections of root, which will be mushy and blackish. Prune back the top of the plant in proportion to the amount of dead and injured root you removed. Then repot the plant in moist soil.

A *Ficus benjamina* or weeping fig sheds its leaves every once in a while. Don't prune back the branches, because new leaves will grow back where the old ones were. However, if the weeping fig continues to shed over a long period of time and nothing new seems to be growing to replace the shedding, check to make sure that your plant has not fallen victim to one of the troubles just described.

Fading leaves

Leaf color fading and eventually turning yellow may mean one of two things. If your plant is also stretching toward the light source and/or the new leaves are smaller and smaller as they appear, your plant may need more light. Multicolored plants like coleus will fade to a dull color if they haven't enough light.

If you think that you are meeting your plant's light requirement but you have fading-leaf trouble, the patient probably needs more nutriment. Feed it more often or check to see that it hasn't outgrown its pot. In the latter event it wouldn't be assimilating needed nutrients because the roots would be too crowded.

Wilted foliage

Foliage sometimes looks dull and wilted. In this case, your plant may be overcrowded in its pot or it may have a shrunken root ball, which means that water isn't penetrating the soil and reaching the roots. Refer to the section on watering in Chapter 4 to see what to do if this is the case. If the plant's home is comfortable and not crowded, check your watering habits; you may have to water more

This waffle plant has developed brown leaf edges because of improper watering habits.

frequently or you may be overwatering. If the soil gets dry between waterings, you're probably not giving the plant enough water as frequently as you should.

Brown leaf edge

A common complaint for many house plants is browning leaf edges. If this is true of your plant, it might want more humidity. Mist more often or put it on a dry well. It is also possible that the plant is being exposed to too much heat or the soil is not being kept moist enough. This is a habitual symptom of the waffle plant.

If there is a white crust on the outside of a clay pot, or a white build-up along the edge of the soil where it meets the inside rim of a clay, plastic, or glazed pot, probably the chemical salts in the soil have increased beyond the proper proportions. Wipe off the white crust and then leach out the excess salts by letting water run through the dirt in the pot. Look back to the beginning of Chapter 3 regarding this leaching process. Piggybacks are particularly susceptible to this kind of damage. One solution for the problem is to water only with rain water or distilled water. This can involve a great deal of trouble, however, so if you periodically leach the soil you may control the problem. Dracaenas and marantas are particularly prone to brown tips from lack of humidity in the air around them. Mist them more often, move them in among companion plants, or set them in a dry-well situation.

Sunburning and water spotting

Foliage that is spotted with glassy yellow or brown patches may have been exposed to too much sun. On the thicker-leaved plants the patches are rather mushy. White or yellow spots on the foilage of some delicate, heavy-leaved plants like the African violet and episcia is often caused by cold water that is spattered or splashed when the plant is watered. Use only tepid water and be careful to only water onto the plant's soil.

Overfertilizing

Blackened and stunted growth is caused by over-fertilizing. There is not much you can do to correct the damage. Just be sure to feed your plant less frequently or with a more diluted solution. If there is a build-up of salts on the pot, wash it off and leach out the soil. Cut off dead and blackened growth.

Bud drop

Flower buds sometimes drop off without blooming; and sometimes a plant that should flower never forms buds at all. There could be many reasons for this: over-watering, underwatering, not enough light, not enough humidity. Flowering plants like a food higher in phosphorus than nitrogen. A high ratio of nitrogen in the fertilizer promotes good foliage growth but blossoms won't get a chance to develop. Some plants, like the African violet, go into a dormant period from about early December until possibly the end of February during which time the flowering slows down and may stop altogether.

Dormant period

Has your plant stopped putting forth new leaves? It may be in its dormant period or resting stage. This usually occurs in the winter months. If, however, it's been more than three months since your plant last grew a new leaf, it may need more light, more food, or a bigger pot. On the other hand, the foliage of plants in pots too large for them sometimes stops growing while the roots work to fill the pot.

Neglect is a frequent cause of plant death; but too much care, that is, *overwatering*, is an even more common cause—and it is such an easy habit to fall into. The best way to avoid drowning your plants is to use your index finger to test the moisture content of the soil before you pour a drop of water. Do be very leery of falling into the overwatering trap.

6 *The Right Tool for the Right Job*

The basic necessities for house plant cultivation are, of course, the plant, a pot, and some soil. However, just as there is a wide variety of pots to select from, there is also a variety of soil elements that can be used. Along with your standard commercial potting soil, you may choose to purchase one or another of the following items to use in addition to the soil, or to mix in with it: charcoal (never briquets, but charcoal for the specific use of aquariums or plants), vermiculite, perlite, builders' sand, peat moss, sphagnum moss, pebbles, bone meal, lime, and any number of other materials may be called for.

Probably the most vital item for plant care is a long-spouted watering can. It is possible to simply carry your plant to the sink and water it from the tap, but if you have quite a few plants, this may become tiresome. This method also involves the risk of splashing the foliage of plants which might cause a bad reaction. This risk is also why a long-spouted watering can is more advantageous than a glass, pitcher, jar, or whatever else may be employed to carry water. The spout can be inserted under or between leaves, thus avoiding any splashes or splatters.

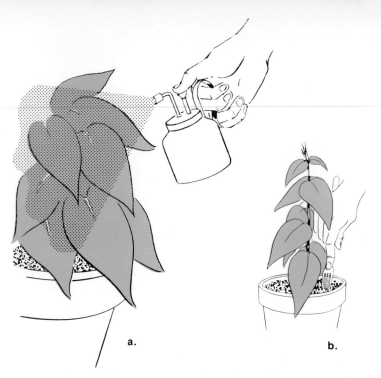

a.

b.

Simple tools to aid the home gardener. (a.) Mister to add humidity to the air around your plant. (b.) Table fork to break up the soil above the plant's root system. (c.) Sharp scissors to trim browning leaf edges. (d.) Sponge to bathe leaves and remove dust film that might cake and prevent plant from breathing.

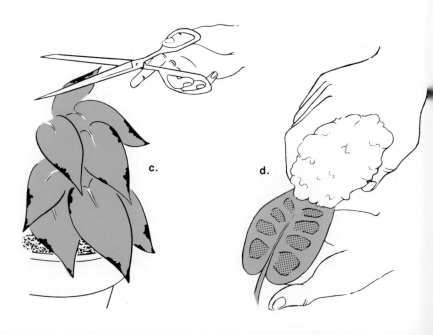

c.

d.

(Possibly a watering can will hold more water, hence fewer trips to the sink.)

Next on your list of needs should be a "mister"—a container with a spray nozzle attached so that a mist of tepid water can be projected over your plants, adding humidity to the air. Misters are available in brass, glass, and functional, but not decorative, plastic. I do not recommend utilizing an empty window cleaner bottle. If there is any residue of ammonia or other cleaning components left in it, real damage to your plants may result. Another disadvantage to using such a bottle is that your finger or thumb will rapidly get worn out from pressing down on the nozzle. The kind of implement made specifically for use on plants releases more spray and finer droplets with each burst.

You may also want to use some kitchen utensils for plant care: a fork, spoon and tongs. The fork will help aerate the soil when the dirt becomes packed down. Then the plant's roots will not only be able to obtain oxygen more easily, but water and nutrients can more rapidly penetrate the surface layers. Don't poke the tines into the soil more than ½ to 1 inch however, or you may end up breaking roots rather than benefiting the plant in any way. So be gentle. The spoon can be used to tamp down soil around a plant after potting by patting the soil with the bowl of the spoon. It can also be employed to help lift a stubborn plant out of a pot. Cactus spines can go right through garden gloves, so it is a practical idea to use tongs for lifting small cacti. A loop of rolled newspaper can be used for grasping larger plants.

Your plant's grooming needs can be aided with a sharp knife, sharp scissors and a sponge. Use the sponge to bathe dust from broad-leaved plants and the scissors to trim off browning leaf edges, yellow leaves or any other unsightly conditions. By virtue of the way in which scissors work, they do pinch the cut surface together, therefore bruising the tissue. In cases of cutting a stalky plant instead of a soft-stemmed plant, it is preferable to use a knife, cutting cleanly and swiftly so that there is no bruising.

You'll also need some fertilizer to replenish food in the soil as your plant uses it up. There are any number of good products on the market. Ask your local plant dealer to recommend one.

Vitamin B-1 can be very beneficial to your plants. It is a great aid when transplanting, rooting cuttings, or caring for sick plants. Another product called root tone is also helpful when you are rooting your cuttings. It stimulates root growth and helps prevent rot.

It is to be hoped that you never find a pesticide necessary. However, if you discover the need for one, read the directions on the label and then read them again. Improper use of insecticides is not only harmful to your plants, but also to other living things, including yourself. Do use caution.

7 Creating with Greenery

Even if you have little or no artistic ability, you can paint a pretty picture with plants simply by situating a few or many together. They can be of the same variety or different types, and can be planted in a terrarium, a dish garden, or just grouped together in their individual pots. Because there are so many sizes, shapes, colors and textures of plants, endless combinations can be made to produce eye-pleasing arrangements. Each plant will look more beautiful by virtue of comparison.

Other than the beautiful accent grouped plants create, you'll probably notice the distinct advantage of better growth. Plants generally enjoy each other's company and thrive in it. They aid each other in producing the humid atmosphere most plants like. The only limitation when grouping plants together is to be careful to only place together those plants that have approximately the same basic needs for light and water. Ferns and cacti will not be a successful combination, but a tiger plant and a cobra plant might do wonders together.

Keeping plants in their own pots enables you to switch an arrangement if you become tired of looking at it. It is also easier to remove ailing plants or to do something about those that may be outgrowing their homes.

A place that you might consider grouping plants to-gether is a corner of your home that could stand some brightening. Large and medium sized plants massed to-gether on an unused hearth during the summer can be quite effective. Do be sure, however, to move them before you build any fires when the weather cools. Different sizes can be beautifully arranged on a table, or on one of any number of plant stands on the market that allows room for several plants. Don't overlook your hanging plants either. They can be grouped together with different lengths of macrame hangers for the added attractiveness of plants hanging at different levels. Or you can group them with standing plants below, creating an eye pleasing line of greenery from floor to ceiling.

You may choose to attempt a topiary design with your plant. Many climbing varieties lend themselves quite well to growing over wire or some other support that is shaped

Plants can be grouped quite effectively on an unused hearth.

Ivy can be trained as a topiary. (a.) Gently tie the plant to a frame. (b.) Keep the vine pinched to encourage lateral growth, and tie each new shoot to the support. (c.) Continue pinching and tying until the frame is covered. Keep the topiary shape controlled by continued pruning.

into an interesting design. For a simple beginning, try growing ivy around a circle of wire. Insert one end of the wire into the soil of the pot, shape it into a circle above the pot, and then place the other end into the soil. Give your plant, or plants, a start in the right direction by tying the shoots gently to the wire with raffia, string, or some other soft material that won't damage the plant's tissue. Green colored raffia is best because it will blend in with the foliage. As the plant grows, continue to tie the new growth to the support. The mesh of chicken wire is excellent for shaping more complicated designs. Cut and bind it into the shape of an animal, and train your plants to cover it. How small or large, or exactly what form, is entirely up to you. Just give your plants time to grow; don't expect them to cover the frame overnight.

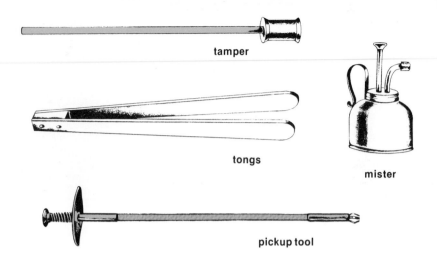

tamper

tongs

mister

pickup tool

If you don't like your pots showing, consider an indoor garden built out of brick, wood, or even wicker lined with plastic. You can set the pots down into them and then cover the pots with either soil, bark or moss. You may even decide to plant directly into the garden if that is easier for you.

On a smaller scale, you might choose to indulge your creative abilities with building a dish garden. As the name implies, the results should be a miniature garden growing in a dish—or actually almost any waterproof container. Four-inch ceramic pots or dishes can house two or three small plants. You can even use a soup bowl, a teacup, a candy dish, or whatever your imagination lights on. Just be sure that you clean it thoroughly before starting your garden. If your container doesn't have drainage holes and you can't make any in it, be sure to put in a layer of pebbles or crock shards first and then a layer of charcoal. Remember to choose plants that like the same kind of environment. Don't put any plant in your dish garden that will quickly grow to huge proportions because it will not only throw your arrangement off balance, but it will crowd

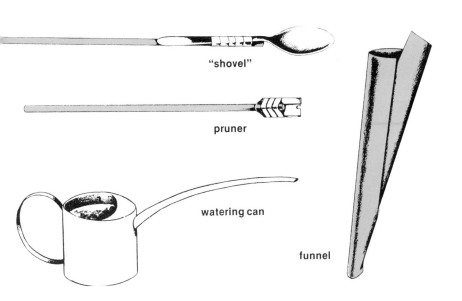

"shovel"

pruner

watering can

funnel

out the other plants. If you make a cacti or succulent garden, be sure to use the proper type of soil. Don't neglect succulents when you are considering which plants to use; they really produce interesting and lovely effects. For a finishing touch, add some pretty pebbles, twigs or other pieces of wood, or ceramic or metal figurines.

Terrariums and bottle gardens are another way to show off plants to an advantage. Somehow, when you view a plant from behind glass, it becomes even more vivid and beautiful. They are really fun to plant and will even present a bit of a challenge, especially if you choose a narrow-necked bottle. A container with an opening large enough to fit your hands (your best tools for planting) into is quite simple to plant; a container with a smaller opening requires a bit of patience, but is even more rewarding when finished because of the little bit of extra effort. This type of garden makes an excellent gift for people who like plants but don't have a lot of time to care for them. They generally need to be watered very infrequently, and then only a small amount. A sealed terrarium may never require water. Once again, use your imagination when choosing a

Planting a terrarium

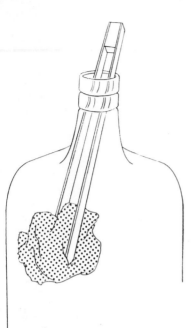

A.

B.

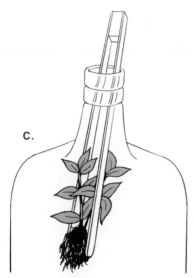

C.

D.

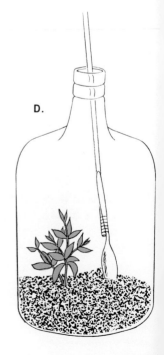

E.

F.

G.

(a.) swabbing glass clean.
(b.) Putting in the soil.
(c.) Placing the plant in.
(d.) Scooping out a place for another plant. (e.) Tamping down the soil. (f.) Pruning a plant. (g.) Using the mister to add water evenly.

container. Almost any clear glass one will do provided it has been thoroughly washed. Try aquarium tanks, fish bowls, brandy snifters, wine bottles, mayonnaise jars, apothecary jars or bubble glasses.

The concept of terrariums was actually hit upon accidentally. Dr. Nathaniel Ward, a nineteenth century English physician, was interested in butterflies and used glass cans to watch the emergence of the butterfly from the cocoon. Evidently, one chrysalis was placed on the glass with a clump of soil, from which green things started to grow. It was then discovered that plants would thrive sometimes for many years enclosed in glass and be very content. Botanists then started to use glass cases to bring back plant specimens from different parts of the world. Now we don't value terrariums for their protective quality as much as for the decoration they provide.

Now go ahead and plant one! It is not very different from planting a dish garden.

Since you are almost surely using a container that has no drainage holes, pebbles or crock shards must first be added to your glass container, then a layer of charcoal to filter the water, and, finally, the soil into which the plants will go. If you are using a narrow-necked bottle, roll a piece of paper into a funnel, insert it into the opening, and add the pebbles, charcoal, and soil through the funnel so that you spread the material evenly and don't dirty the glass sides. Make hills and dales with the soil if you wish; it doesn't have to be evenly flat. With a long handled ice tea spoon, a spoon tied to a stick by the handle, or just a blunt ended stick, scoop out holes where you intend to place your plants. Hopefully, you've chosen plants that are relatively slow growing and that like a lot of humidity and moist soil. Knock them out of their pots, and gently shake most of the soil from their roots. Then with your choice of any number of tools—chopsticks, a piece of bamboo split

A lovely garden that is also a balanced ecosystem.

at one end, long-handled tweezers, or a special metal pickup tool (found in hardware stores and costing less than $2.00), lower your plants into their designated spots.

With a blunt-ended stick, gently tamp the soil down around the plants' roots. If any soil has been dropped on the foliage, brush it off with an artist's paint brush. Give your garden a couple of sprays with your mister to insure moist soil, and then if you wish add some decorative pieces, like pebbles, twigs, or little figurines. If you want to clean the sides of your container, attach a piece of cloth or soft paper to a stick and carefully swab the sides.

In a large terrarium, like one made out of an aquarium, you might like to add a live lizard or snake for an extra bit of interest. Pick an animal that won't grow too large for the terrarium and be sure to feed it the proper type of food so that it can remain happy and healthy within the balanced ecology of your terrarium.

Now cover or cork up your landscape in miniature and put it in a cool, low-lit place for a couple of days while the plants adjust to their new environment. After that, you may then move it where you wish; just don't put it in bright light or direct sunlight. If big droplets of moisture collect on the glass, or the container is so steamed up that you can't see inside, take off the cover for a little while to let some of the moisture evaporate. Then replace the cover.

If you find the need to prune your plants or cut off any yellowing or dying vegetation, use a single-edged razor blade taped to a stick. Chopsticks or long-handled tweezers can be used to remove the prunings.

Your terrariums should remain beautiful and thrive with a minimum of maintenance.

8 Growing New From Old

Half the fun of house plant cultivation is the satisfaction of starting new plants from mature, established ones. Not only is it gratifying to watch a plant that you started grow to become a good-sized member of its species, but you may soon acquire so many that giving them to friends can become a source of pleasure too. There are several methods of propagation, so be sure to use the one that is best suited to your particular plant.

Stem cuttings

With sharp scissors, cut four or five inches of stem from your plant below a leaf joint or node, which is where roots form. This snipping should include at least four leaves. Strip the leaves from the lower portion of the stem, which will be below the level of the water or rooting medium. The leaves you cut off would only rot and spread trouble to the entire cutting. If you wish, you can dip the end of the stem in a rooting hormone powder, one that promotes rapid root growth and prevents fungus growth, but it's not really necessary. Of course, if you are rooting in water, the hormone will just wash off.

You can root in water or a porous medium like vermiculite or perlite which holds moisture, or a mixture of

a.

b.

one of these with peat or chopped sphagnum moss, sand, or even potting soil. The solid mediums must be kept constantly moist until the roots of the cutting are well developed. In order of personal preference I would list the vermiculite/perlite or moss mixture, then sand, potting soil, and finally plain water. Roots form faster in water, but they are sturdier if they are allowed to develop in a substantial medium. There is also the fact that they must make an adjustment all over again when you transfer them from the water to soil when you finally pot them.

However, for many people rooting a cutting in water is the easiest procedure. Simply cover the opening of a drinking glass or a jar, preferably an opaque one, with aluminum foil or plastic wrap and insert the stem of your cutting into a hole poked through the foil or plastic. The leaves will be supported by this covering so that they won't be submerged in water to encourage rot. Replenish the water as it evaporates.

If you choose one of the other methods, be sure your medium is moist, then poke a hole in it with a pencil or stick, insert your cutting about two inches deep, and gently settle the soil around it. When planting more than

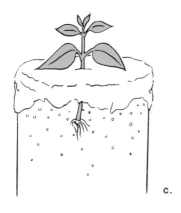

c.

d.

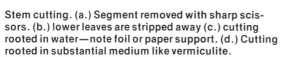

Stem cutting. (a.) Segment removed with sharp scissors. (b.) lower leaves are stripped away (c.) cutting rooted in water—note foil or paper support. (d.) Cutting rooted in substantial medium like vermiculite.

one cutting in the same container, be sure not to let the leaves touch one another. It is also a good idea to slip a plastic bag around pot and cutting, mist the cutting, blow into the bag to fill it with air so that the plastic doesn't come into contact with the cutting, and tie it off. Keep it out of direct sunlight. If big drops of water form, open the bag for a few hours to let the water evaporate a little and then close it again. Roots should form in about ten days. You can determine if they have or not by pulling gently at the cutting. If it resists, you probably have roots. Now you should keep the bag open to let air in, but don't take the plant out for a few days so it can adjust from a terrarium-like humidity to a drier atmosphere.

Plants which root easily from stem cuttings include most trailing plants like ivy, wandering jew, and purple velvet. Some upright plants, like the coleus and pilea varieties, also develop roots easily. Succulents like the jade plant and some cacti will root from cuttings but the cuttings should be allowed to dry out for several days before they are put into the rooting medium, which is moist sand. This period of drying permits a callus to form at the break, which discourages rotting.

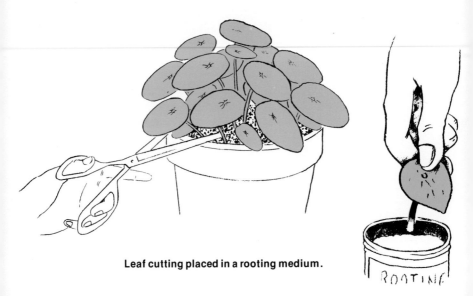

Leaf cutting placed in a rooting medium.

ROOTING

Leaf cuttings

Rooting a leaf cutting is very similar to the method used for a stem cutting. Choose a medium-sized leaf; little ones are too young and old ones tend to rot. Cut it from the plant with sharp scissors, including at least one inch of the leaf stem or petiole. Follow the same procedure described for rooting a cutting, whether you choose to root it in water or a soil medium. It will probably take from one to two months to root. African violets and peperomias root easily this way.

Most succulents will root easily from only a leaf. To repeat: let the leaf dry for several days to discourage rotting. Succulent leaves should be rooted in moist sand.

A piggyback leaf does best if you cut off the entire stem, roll it into a funnel shape, and insert one third of the entire leaf in a rooting medium.

Another method of leaf cutting involves cutting a leaf into segments and planting each piece. You can do this

(a.) Sanseveria plant (b.) Leaf cut into segments (c.) Cutting placed in rooting medium and covered with plastic bag to retain humidity (d.) New baby plant.

with the fleshy-leaved sansevieria. Cut the leaf into pieces about three inches long and insert each piece by the base into a pot of moist rooting medium. Then bag the pot and keep it out of the sun for a few weeks. When the new shoot is a few inches high, cut off the old piece.

Similar to this is the rooting of a rex begonia from leaf segments. Cut the leaf so that each piece includes a main vein and a bit of the stem. Lay the piece on the top of a moist rooting medium and staple it down over the vein with hairpins or pieces of bent wire. Then bag the pot and wait. It could take a couple of months.

Soil layering

Soil layering is a simple method of propagation. String of beads is easy to propagate this way. Just bury about one inch of the stem at any point in moist soil. Three or four weeks later some roots should have developed. Now just cut the two plants apart and repot.

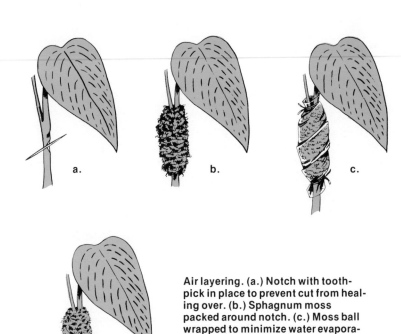

Air layering. (a.) Notch with toothpick in place to prevent cut from healing over. (b.) Sphagnum moss packed around notch. (c.) Moss ball wrapped to minimize water evaporation. (d.) Roots developing in moss.

Air layering

For stalky plants like dieffenbachia and dracaena, air layering is the best propagation method. Notch the stem about halfway through just below a leaf node. Put a toothpick in the cut to prevent it from healing over, and pack moist sphagnum moss in and around it. Wrap the moss with plastic wrap and tie it in place above and below the wad of moss. Check periodically to see that the moss remains moist. In a couple of months you should see roots. Cut off the new plant and pot it. If you continue to water the old stalks as usual, new leaves will eventually sprout.

Runners

Some plants put out runners. These are individual plantlets that are not quite completely formed. If you put them in contact with moist soil or moss, they should develop roots and can then be separated from the mother plant. Do this by placing little satellite pots around the mother plant and setting the plantlets on the soil in them. You should soon have well-developed baby plants that you can then separate from the large plant. You can also simply cut the plantlets off and root them in water, but that method is not as certain and doesn't produce plants as strong. Spider plant and strawberry begonia are good examples of plants that put out runners.

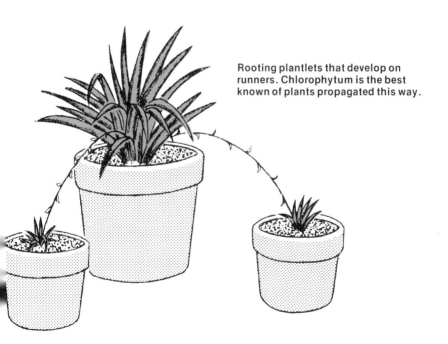

Rooting plantlets that develop on runners. Chlorophytum is the best known of plants propagated this way.

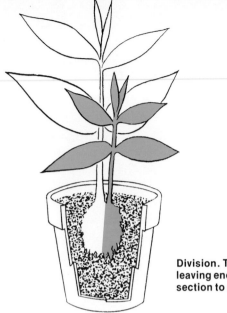

Division. The root ball is separated, leaving enough root and stem in each section to develop a healthy plant.

Division and offsets

Another way to get a new plant from a mature one is by division. This seems to work best for ferns and plants that develop two or more main stems like sansevieria, cast-iron, Chinese evergreen and some cacti.

When dividing ferns, simply cut through the root mass with a sharp knife, making sure that each part has some of the fleshy roots, then repot each part.

When dividing plants like the cast-iron plant, get the plant out of the pot and gently remove most of the dirt around the roots. Now cut the two plants apart nearest the mother plant and repot each. African violets and peperomias form two or more crowns. These can be divided in the same way to make separate plants.

After you have potted a newly developed plant, don't feed it until it is well established. That should be when its pot is well filled with roots. The chemicals in any fertilizer you feed the plant may be too strong for a poorly developed root system.

9 *When You're On Vacation*

The easiest way to eliminate vacation plant care worries is to have a knowledgeable and reliable friend look after your plants. Lacking that, even a not-so-knowledgeable friend is pretty nice to have around. Just be sure to chart a watering schedule for each plant and label every one of your plants so that when she reads "water the monkey plant every Monday, Wednesday and Friday," she doesn't faithfully follow directions and drown your favorite cactus. Another possibility is to hire a plant sitter. Look in your local newspaper for ads.

However, don't get discouraged if these methods aren't possible; there are alternatives that work almost as well.

The first thing to do before leaving is thoroughly water every plant and then let them drain. If you have only a couple of plants, you may want to buy one of the commercial watering aids. These devices work on the principle that moisture will travel through a cotton wick, one end of which is absorbing water from a container while its other end is inserted in the plant's soil. If you don't have an outrageous number of plants like I do, you can create a terrarium atmosphere by bagging each plant in a clear plas-

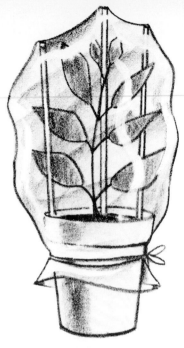

Plants can be placed in plastic bags to create a terrarium-like atmosphere. This makes it possible to vacation without worrying about watering them.

tic bag. Simply set the pot in a bag, blow it up to fill it with air and to keep the plastic from collapsing on the plant tissue which may cause rot, and then close it with rubber bands. If it looks like the foliage is touching plastic, wrap it again, this time using bamboo sticks inserted in the plant's soil to prop the bag away from the plant. For many plants, set them in your sinks and then cover them with plastic wrap propped up with bamboo sticks and tape the plastic down on all sides so that you have a tent-like structure. The same thing can be done for large plants in the bathtub using dry-cleaning bags, or you may wrap them individually.

Remember that your plants cannot survive in darkness so leave a curtain open for them. If you'd rather not do that, do leave some bright lights on. It is even better if the lights are attached to timers so that you can simulate the day/night cycle. Timers on lights are also good investments to discourage prospective burglars.

10 Bromeliads— Living Pitchers

Bromeliads make wonderful house plants. Not only are they colorful, unusual—sometimes even bizarre—and for the most part, very easy to grow, but they also have gloriously beautiful blooms. Few European households are without a bromeliad. They seem to be favorite candidates for house plants among our overseas friends.

Technically herbs because they grow no woody tissue, bromeliads are native to the Western Hemisphere, with the exception of one lone species that originated on the west coast of Africa. The rest are found in the Southern United States, the Caribbean, and Central and South America. Of about 2,000 species, probably the most familiar are the common pineapple and Spanish moss.

The majority of these plants grow in the form of a rosette, with the center forming a cup that should always be at least partially filled with water. In their natural habitat these wells of water often serve as a complete microcosm, hosting bacteria, algae and protozoans which in turn support insects that serve as food for frogs and spiders. It has also been reported that the water held by bromeliads was invaluable to the early explorers of Florida's Everglades who survived droughts by drinking from the plant's cup.

Bromeliads need to have their cups kept filled with water.

Bromeliads are epiphytic rather than parasitic. That means that although they may cling to a tree, they do not feed from it, but instead they gather some nutriment from rotting vegetation trapped in the host plant's nooks and crannies. They also gather food and moisture from the atmosphere itself. Some bromeliads, like the pineapple, grow from the ground, but most perch high on trees and cliffs. Sometimes a heavy rain will fill their cups until the extra weight of the water causes them to loose their grip and come tumbling down.

Most bromeliads like a moist atmosphere, but some prefer a desert-like climate. The latter type absorb moisture from the atmosphere through microscopic scales that coat their leaves. You can pot your bromeliad or plant it on a piece of bark or a branch by wrapping the roots in sphagnum moss filled with the type of growing medium they prefer—or even just the moss—attaching it with chicken wire to the wood. Bromeliads like a coarse

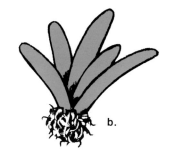

Bromeliads can be grown quite successfully on a piece of bark or driftwood. (a.) Take a plant out of its pot with the root ball intact. (b.) Wrap the root ball with moist sphagnum moss. (c.) Attach it to the wood with chicken wire.

growing medium; equal parts of sphagnum or peat moss and sand and soil will serve well. Most of these plants like bright light, warmth, high humidity, barely moist soil, and continuously water filled cups; however, many of them will tolerate far less than ideal situations. For the most part, misting is appreciated except when they are in bloom. At that time misting may shorten the flower's life.

The bromeliad rosette blooms just once and afterwards develops a side shoot that blooms again one to three years later. This may seem like an awfully long time to wait for a flower, but keep in mind that the flower is extremely long lasting—up to five months—and it is extremely impressive. (A daffodil blossom may last only a week or two, and you wait a year to see it.) If a plant doesn't seem to want to bloom, and it appears to be healthy, try closing it in a plastic bag along with a couple of apples for two days. The ethylene gas produced by the apples may encourage flower formation.

A variegated *Ananas*.

Aechmea

This bromeliad is called the living vase plant because of its ability to hold water. One popular variety, *A. fasciata*, is native to Brazil and grows about 1½ feet tall and flowers in late summer. Propagate from offsets.

Ananas comosus

This plant is the common pineapple. It likes a high level of humidity so be sure to mist it frequently. Propagate from a ripe pineapple fruit by grasping the leaves and twisting the top off. You may either root it in water or let it dry for a few days and pot it directly into a growing medium.

Billbergia

B. nutans is a very popular variety because it is easy to grow and produces beautiful flowers. Keep it moist in the summer, but let the soil dry out between waterings in the winter. Propagate from offsets.

85

One of the many varieties of *Aechmea*.

This *Neoregelia* has produced two good sized pups.

Cryptanthus

This bromeliad's name means hidden flower. Unlike most bromeliads that grow flowers on tall stalks, this one blooms almost beneath its leaves. It is low growing, hence the nickname earthstars. *Cryptanthus zonatus* will change color from green to brown depending upon how much light it does or does not receive. Propagate from offsets.

Neoregelia

The variety *N. carolinae tricolor* from Brazil is really quite beautiful. Its wiry striped green leaves become rose tinted in spring; this hue may last through autumn. Propagate from offsets.

87

The colorful *Cryptanthus*.

Here, a *Vriesia* dwarfs its relative, *Tillandsia*

Tillandsia

This bromeliad is quite handsome when it is grown on bark as a hanging rosette. Its dark green, rather narrow leaves grow downward instead of up as most other bromeliads. Like the others, it produces spectacular flower bracts and flowers. Propagate from offsets or pups, as they are often called.

Vriesia

This bromeliad is colorful and compact. Some of its varieties are nicknamed flaming swords because they develop bright red flower spikes. Propagate from offsets or remove the new plant that may grow in the center of the old.

11 *Cacti and Other Succulent Plants*

Cacti are part of a large group of plants called succulents. Through the process of evolution the cacti species lost their leaves which allowed too much precious moisture to evaporate into the dry desert air. Their stems became thick and rounded enabling the plants to store the scarce water. Many species developed a hairy covering or sharp spines as protection against the sun's hot rays and against hungry, thirsty animals that might view the plants as a juicy meal. For the most part, succulents evolved under less severe conditions and developed thick, fleshy leaves covered with a waxy or scale-like material to reduce moisture evaporation from the leaf surface.

As house plant specimens, these plants should certainly not be overlooked. The variety of shapes, sizes and colors is simply amazing.

Some succulents are short and squat like the cactus genera *Astrophytum*, while others are tremendously tall like the saguaro cactus which may grow to heights of 50 feet or more. Then there are those that trail, like the *Sedum* variety, donkey's tail, and even some that closely resemble stones, like many *Lithops* varieties. Many species bloom brilliantly.

Besides the advantageous huge selection to choose from, succulents present the added benefits of being extremely easy to grow, tolerant of neglect, and generally disease and pest resistant.

They are, however, rather slow growing. They definitely require bright light for survival, so reserve your brightest area for these plants. Remember to turn them occasionally so that all sides of each plant receive equal attention from the sun. But don't move a plant that is ready to bloom as it may cause the buds to drop. They are very sensitive at this stage and any disturbance, such as movement or a change in light degree, will upset them.

If you plan to summer your succulents out-of-doors, keep in mind two things. The first is, as strange as it may sound, the plants may burn in full sunlight and the heat of a summer afternoon; they have become acclimated to the less than perfect amount of light indoors. It would be best to move them to a slightly shaded area during the afternoons. Second, look carefully for any pests your plant may be harboring when you decide to bring it back into the house. A good way to check for this is to immerse the bottom half of the plant's pot in water and see if anything rises to the surface of the soil.

Now a word about watering these plants: *seldom*— that is, be very careful not to overwater. Let the soil dry out between waterings during the growing season and water even less in their dormant periods (from about November to February). Throughout the dormant period water just enough to keep the plant from shriveling. Don't water at all on humid days. Water is not taken in as rapidly by the plant's roots, nor does it evaporate as quickly, and the result may be a rotted plant. Never use cold water which shocks the plant's system.

Because of the succulent's preference for dry conditions, good drainage and aeration are essential. Keep this in mind when you repot a plant and add some coarse gravel and a layer of charcoal to the bottom of the pot. Contrary to popular belief, succulents do not like to live in pure sand. A good soil combination for them is equal parts of commercial potting soil and builders' sand (never sea sand—the salt will burn the plant) and the addition of one tablespoon of bone meal to each gallon of soil for nutriment and one tablespoon of ground limestone to each gallon to assure the alkaline conditions. If you find it difficult to recall what type of soil your plant likes—acid or alkaline—remember that most plants in low rainfall areas like an alkaline soil and most in regions with higher amounts of rainfall like an acid soil. The bone meal you added is a slow-acting fertilizer that will last throughout the year. When you add more nutrients at the end of the year, remember that succulents grow slowly so it is a good idea to dilute your house plant fertilizer to one half of the recommended strength.

The best time of the year to repot these plants is in the early spring when maximum growth is in progress so that they can divide their energies to include adjusting to new surroundings. Don't repot into too large of a container; succulents have shallow roots and the larger the pot, the more soil that will absorb water and take longer to evaporate, and the more likely you are to overwater. When handling cacti, don't forget those with spines can be harmful. Some spines will go right through garden gloves, so it is a good practice to use tongs to handle the smaller plants and rolled newspaper to grasp the larger ones. After potting, tamp the soil down and give the pot a quick thump on a solid surface to settle the soil and eliminate air pockets that may cause water to run down the insides of the pot instead of reaching the plant's roots. *Do not* water the plant for several days after repotting.

Cacti and succulents are easy to propagate by means of division, stem or leaf cuttings. Refer to Chapter 8 for more information.

Some cacti have gorgeous flowers, but it can sometimes be tricky to get them to bloom. Optimum conditions to induce blossoms include a cool temperature during the plant's resting period. Try putting it in an unheated garage or porch at night if the temperature does not drop below freezing. Lacking that, place them close to a glass window at night where the temperature is quite a bit lower than in the middle of a room. Cactus flowers last only a short time but they are worth any extra effort, as they are truly spectacular.

A unique cactus has been created
by the process known as "grafting".

Cacti are unique in the respect that they can be grafted. This is a process by which a plant or stem section of a plant is joined to the rooted stem of another, different plant. Here is another way to utilize your creative genius with plants and come up with singular results. As with repotting, this is best done in the spring. Grafting is explained simply in the following steps:

With a knife, sterilized in alcohol, cut off the top of the cactus you intend to use as the base. Bevel the top downward. This trims spines out of the way and assures that the second plant you are grafting on will not be lifted off as the cut dries. Sterilize your knife again and make a thin, flat slice along the top, and leave the slice in place to keep the wound moist.

(b.) Cut off roots of plant to be used for the top, and bevel the cut upward.

(a.) Cut off top of plant to be used for base. Bevel the top downward.

(c.) Put plants together with growth rings matching and secure with rubber bands or weighted strings.

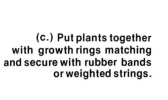

Unpot the plant that you are going to use for the upper part (called *scion*) and slice off its roots. Bevel the edge upward. Again, with a sterilized knife make a thin slice along the top and leave the slice in place.

Just before you press together the scion and the stalk, discard the protective slices. Be sure the two plants are lined up with their central growth rings matching to guarantee the flow of food and water between the two plants. Secure the plants in place with rubber bands or strings weighted with hardware nuts draped over the top. This is necessary not only to hold them together, but to add a slight pressure which will force out any air bubbles that might allow bacteria to enter. Do not water the plant or put it in the sun for a few days until the graft takes. Then remove the strings or rubber bands and enjoy your new plant.

Two forms of *Aloe*

Agave
A. filfera, A. picta, A. victoriae-reginae

This succulent has been given the nickname century plant—so called because it takes so long to bloom. Actually it is not a century between blooming seasons, but sometimes it can be fifty years before it blossoms again. Most century plants grow to become too large for household decoration; the above-listed varieties are fine as house plants, however, because they are very slow growing.

Aloe
A. variegata—tiger aloe, *A. vera*—true aloe, *A. ristata*—lace aloe

This succulent is a member of the lily family. It blooms in the winter.

Astrophytum ornatum

Aporocactus flagelliformis

This cactus, originally from Mexico, is called the rat-tail cactus because of its slender hanging stems. It produces a red flower.

Astrophytum

A. asterias—sand dollar, *A. myriostigma*—Bishop's cap

The sand dollar cactus consists of eight segments forming a low dome and has no spines. It produces yellow flowers with red throats. The Bishop's cap consists of five segments forming a star shape, and it is covered with soft white scales. It produces yellow flowers.

Different varieties of the *Crassula* genus planted in a dish garden for a lovely arrangement.

Cephalocereus senilis

This cactus is called the old man cactus because it is covered with long white hair-like spines. Its original habitat is Mexico. It produces a rose-colored flower.

Crassula

C. Portulacea—jade plant, *C. arborescens*—silver dollar plant

There are many, many varieties of the *crassula* family. Some of them take the form of miniature trees.

Echinocereus

E. armatus—hedgehog cactus, *E. dasyacanthus*—rainbow cactus

This species is of small stature and is extremely easy to grow—it also easily cultivates flowers. It blooms in colors of red, purple, pink, yellow and white in the summer season.

Haworthia

H. fasciata—zebra haworthia, *H. margaritifera*—pearly haworthia

This succulent has a black surface that is marked in various patterns with a raised growth called tubercles.

Lithops

There are many varieties of this charming succulent. Most resemble pebbles or stones, and produce a flower from the division in the center of the plant.

Lobivia

L. aurea—golden Easter lily cactus, *L. famatimensis*—orange cob cactus

This small cactus is an easy to grow species. The two varieties listed produce beautiful flowers in early summer.

Mammillaria

M. bocasana—powder puff cactus, *M. camptotricha*—bird's nest cactus, *M. candida*—snowball pincushion, *M. elongata*—golden star cactus

There are many varieties of this cactus. It produces young plants in clusters around the parent plant. It flowers in the winter and spring.

Lobivia

Two varieties of the *Mammilaria* genus, *M. macdougali* and *M. elongata* "golden stars".

Opuntia

O. basilaris—beavertail cactus, *O. glomerata*—paper-spine cactus, *O. microdasys*—bunny ears

These species of cactus are divided into two types, the prickly pear and the cholla. The prickly pears have pad shaped sectional stems and no spines; they have instead clusters of bristles 1/16 inch long called glochida that can really hurt if you happen to get pricked. The cholla type has cylindrical branches joined together link fashion, and some very mean spines. The first and third varieties listed are of the prickly pear type. Most varieties of this species grow very large, but these listed grow neither too tall nor too fast and make good house plants.

Pachyphytum

Pachyphytum

P. bractiosum—silver tract, *P. oviferum*—moonstones

    This succulent is very easy to grow and never gets too tall. The silver tract may grow to twelve inches, and moonstones grows about six inches high.

Rebutia

    This cactus is originally from Argentina. It is globular in shape and bears large blooms all around its base—hence the name crown cactus.

Sedum morganianum
This succulent, commonly known as donkey's tail, should be placed where it won't be brushed against as its leaves are easily dislodged.

A Pictorial
Encyclopedia
of House Plants

Abutilion

The flowering maple is truly a colorful, graceful plant. It has the added advantage of blooming fairly continuously in shades of white, yellow, orange, pink or red, depending on the variety. But it does require a bright light, or even some sun, to produce flowers. It likes evenly moist soil, and, because it is a rapid grower, it likes to be fed on a regular schedule. Prune to control the shape of this plant. *Abutilion* belongs to the plant family, *Malvaceae.* Propagate from stem cuttings.

Acorus japonicus

As its name indicates, the unusual Japanese sweet flag comes from Japan. It likes to be kept evenly moist in a bright to medium light. *Acorus* prefers a cool temperature, but it is a hardy plant and will tolerate a warm climate. This plant is excellent for use in dish gardens and terrariums. *Acorus* belongs to the *Araceae* family. Propagate by dividing.

Aeschynanthus

The most common varieties of this plant are *A. speciosus* and *A. lobbianus,* the lipstick plants, and *A. marmoratus,* the black pagoda plant. The two lipstick plants come from Java; *A. speciosus* has larger leaves. The black pagoda plant comes from Siam. Its leaves are similar to *A. speciosus* except that they are marked with maroon on the undersides. All of these plants bloom—the lipstick produces red-orange flowers, and the black pagoda, which blooms more infrequently, produces a greenish flower. All *Aeschynanthus* need a bright light for good growth and to develop their spectacular flowers. The soil should constantly be kept barely moist, and a high level of humidity should be provided for best results. Prune your plant back in early spring or late winter before new growth begins to encourage prolific blossoms the following spring—flowers only develop in new growth. *Aeschynanthus* belongs to the *Gesneriaceae* family. (Therefore, it is a relative of the African violet.) Propagate from stem cuttings.

Alsophila australis

The Australian tree fern is a hardy plant from Tasmania and Australia. It may grow up to 20 feet high, but not so rapidly that you will be pushed out of your home. It is, however, generally sold as a large plant which is best set off in a spacious foyer or room. This tree fern likes a medium light and soil that is constantly kept quite moist. It prefers warmth. *Alsophila* belongs to the *Dicksoniaceae* family.

Alternanthera versicolor

The colorful butterfly leaf or Joseph's coat is from Brazil. It is relatively low growing and compact; therefore, it is a good specimen for use in dish gardens and terrariums. Butterfly leaf needs a bright light and evenly moist soil. It prefers a warm temperature. Keep this plant pinched to encourage bushy growth. *Alternanthera* is a member of the family, *Amaranthaceae.* Propagate from stem cuttings.

Arabian sea grape: see *Cissus*

Areca palm: see *Chrysalidocarpus*

Asparagus

Many varieties of asparagus "ferns" are fairly common, but there are a couple that are frequently overlooked, *A. falcatus* and *A. splendens*. The *falcatus* is exceptionally easy to grow. *Asparagus splendens* is not difficult by any means, but, like the better-known *sprengeri* variety, it does tend to shed somewhat indoors. It looks a good deal like the *sprengeri*, but it has smaller, more delicately formed leaves (or needles). It climbs and twines up and around supports quite readily. The asparagus ferns like evenly moist soil and medium to bright light. Propagate by dividing. They belong to the *Liliaceae* family.

Australian tree fern: see *Alsophila*

Balfour aralia: see *Polyscias*

Bamboo: see *Nandina*

Beaucarnea recurvata

The unusual elephant foot tree or bottle palm is very easy to grow. Your only difficulty in cultivating this plant is in having enough space—it can grow up to 30 feet tall. But don't worry, it's not a particularly rapid grower. The bottle palm requires a bright light and soil that is allowed to dry out between waterings. The fat base of the plant, which gives the plant its nickname, stores water. A yearly feeding is recommended for this plant. Just use your average house plant fertilizer. Bottle palm is a member of the *Liliaceae* family.

Beloperone guttata

This plant from Mexico is nicknamed shrimp plant because the flower bracts it produces do resemble shrimp. One variety has copper-colored flower bracts; the other has yellow. Keep this plant pruned so that it doesn't become leggy. The shrimp plant likes a bright light—even some sun—and soil that is allowed to dry out slightly between waterings. Propagate from stem cuttings. *Beloperone* belongs to the *Acanthaceae* family.

Black pagoda: see *Aeschynanthus*

Blizzard vine: see *Glecoma*

Bottle palm: see *Beaucarnea*

Butterfly leaf: see *Alternanthera*

Butterfly palm: see *Chysalidocarpus*

Capsicum annum

There are many varieties of the ornamental pepper plant, with differing colors, sizes and shapes of edible peppers. Treat this interesting plant as an annual because, although they may live more than one year, they often become straggly and unattractive. These plants like a sunny or bright location and evenly moist soil. Ornamental peppers are members of the *Solanaceae* family. Propagate from seeds.

Chamaerops humilis

Most palms are easy to grow, but the European fan palm is exceptionally sturdy. It is sometimes sold for outdoor use, but it makes an excellent house plant. It won't get much bigger than six feet, so you don't have to worry about it eventually lifting your roof. The fan palm prefers a bright light, but will tolerate a medium light. Keep its soil very moist at all times, but provide good drainage. This plant prefers a cool temperature. It belongs to the *Palmae* family. Propagate from offsets.

Chinese podocarpus: see *Podocarpus*

Chrysalidocarpus lutescens

The butterfly palm is also known as the Areca palm. It is particularly popular because it grows in clusters rather than single stems. This plant prefers a bright light but will tolerate a medium light. Keep its soil very moist, but be sure it has good drainage. Propagate by dividing the clumps. This palm belongs to the family *Palmae*.

Cissus rotundifolia

The remarkably hardy Arabian sea grape is rather unusual. Related to the grape and kangaroo ivies, it doesn't resemble them in the least. It is a vining plant like the others, but its foliage is rounded and of a more succulent nature. It can be maintained as an upright plant or allowed to trail. Let the soil dry out moderately between waterings. It prefers a medium to bright light, but will tolerate a low light. Propagate from stem cuttings. The *Cissus* is a member of the *Vitaceae* family.

Clerodendrum thomsonae

This tropical plant's natural habitat is West Africa. It is a climber or trailer that produces beautiful white and crimson flowers in the spring. It likes a bright light and evenly moist soil. The *Clerodendrum* prefers warmth. It belongs to the *Verbenaceae* family. Propagate from cuttings.

Cobra plant: see *Darlingtonia*

Cobra plant: see *Lamium*

Coffea arabica

The coffee plant is a rather tricky one to grow successfully, but its shiny green foliage makes it quite attractive. It can also be an interesting item of conversation, especially if it produces coffee "beans" when mature. The coffee plant prefers bright light, a warm temperature, and soil that is kept barely moist. It belongs to the *Rubiaceae* family.

Coffee plant: see *Coffea arabica*

Coprosma baueri variegata

The colorful leaves of the mirror plant are very attractive. They appear to have been polished to a very high gloss, so shiny are they. The mirror plant is very easy to grow. It likes a bright to medium light and evenly moist soil. Its natural habitat is New Zealand. *Coprosma* is a member of the *Rubiaceae* family.

Creeping jenny: see *Lysimachia*

Cyanotis somuliensis

The emerald elf vine or pussy ears originated in India. It likes a bright light and soil that is allowed to dry out moderately between waterings. *Cyanotis* is fun to touch because of the soft, fuzzy texture of the leaves. It produces purple or orange flowers. However, it is not one of the easiest plants to grow; it is brittle and easily broken, and it likes neither too much water nor to have water poured directly onto the foliage. But its beauty makes it worth the extra trouble. Propagate from stem cuttings. *Cyanotis* is a member of the *Commelinaceae* family.

Cymbalaria muralis

The Kennilworth Ivy is from Germany, France and Switzerland. It is a lovely, delicate-looking trailing plant which produces a profusion of small white flowers. It likes a medium light and evenly moist soil. The Kennilworth Ivy belongs to the *Scrophulariaceae* family. Propagate by dividing—it will spread to fill a container.

Cyperus

The umbrella plant is native to Madagascar. *C. alternifolius* may grow to four feet, but the dwarf variety, *C. gracilis,* grows only to two feet. *Cyperus* is frequently grown for outdoor use, but it makes an excellent house plant. The umbrella plant—not to be confused with *Schefflera* which is also called umbrella plant—requires a medium to bright light and wet soil. (It's a great plant for those of you that tend to overwater.) Propagate by dividing. This plant is one of the preferred meals of the spider mite, so discourage an invasion with fresh air, cleanliness, and frequent mistings. *Cyperus* belongs to the *Cyperaceae* family.

Darlingtonia californica

The carnivorous cobra plant is native to the bogs in California and Oregon. It traps insects in its hood which secretes a sweet, sticky substance to attract victims. The cobra plant likes a rich, wet soil; add chopped sphagnum moss to commercial potting soil to aid in retaining water. High humidity and a medium to low light are preferred. It is not necessary to feed the cobra plant flies or insects; it will subsist on the nutrients in the soil. However, it will grow more luxuriously on a diet of animal protein. The cobra plant belongs to the *Sarraceniaceae* family.

Dipladenia sanderi rosea

This plant, whose natural home is Brazil, produces salmon pink and yellow flowers throughout the year. *Dipladenia* requires a bright light and soil that is allowed to dry out slightly between waterings. It prefers a warm temperature and a high level of humidity. Propagate from stem cuttings. This plant belongs to the *Apocynaceae* family. Prune if the plant requires it in the early spring.

Drosera filiformis

The carnivorous sundew is native to North America. It traps insects in the curving hairs on its leaves. It likes a very moist soil, high humidity, and a bright light. Add chopped sphagnum moss to commercial potting soil to assure that moisture is retained. The sundew does not need to be fed live insects; it will live off nutrients in the soil. However, it will grow better if insects are included in its diet. It belongs to the *Droseraceae* family.

Elephant foot tree: see *Beaucarnea*

Emerald elf vine: see *Cyanotis*

Euonymus japonicus

There are many varieties of *Euonymus japonicus;* the Pearl Edge, Silver Queen, and Yellow Queen are some. They differ basically in the green shades of the leaf, and the color and width of the leaf margin. These plants are easy to grow and require only a medium to bright light and evenly moist soil. They prefer a cool temperature and appreciate misting. Control your plant's shape with pinching and pruning. *Euonymus* belongs to the *Celastreaceae* family. Propagate from stem cuttings.

European fan palm: see *Chamaerops*

False holly: see *Osmanthus*

Fire fern: see *Oxalis*

Fivefingers: see *Nothopanax*

Flowering maple: see *Abutilion*

German ivy: see *Senecio*

127

Glecoma hederacea

The creeping blizzard vine is a little difficult to make flourish, but it can be a charming hanging plant. It produces blue flowers, and the variegated form has white leaf margins. The blizzard vine's natural habitat is Europe and Asia. It likes a medium to bright light and evenly moist soil. It may want to be watered very frequently. Propagate from cuttings or by dividing. It belongs to the family *Labiatae*.

Goldfish plant: see *Hypocyrta*

Grevillea robusta

The foliage of the relatively rapid-growing silk oak resembles that of a fern, although the silk oak is actually a tree. It is an easy plant to grow; all it requires is a bright light—even some sun— and soil that is allowed to dry out moderately between waterings. However, it does not care for sudden changes in temperature and will show its displeasure by dropping leaves. Its native habitat is Queensland and New South Wales. You may choose to prune this plant in early spring to control its shape, but pruning isn't a necessity. The *Grevillea* belongs to the *Proteaceae* family.

Hanging velvet vine: see *Mikania*

Hemigraphis exotica

The waffle plant is a beautiful trailing variety, particularly lovely when suspended. This easy-to-grow plant comes from New Guinea. Its metallic purple underleaf color is an excellent foil for green plants. The waffle plant likes to be kept constantly moist; it will flop like the piggyback when it dries out. Try not to let that happen. It will tolerate a low light, but a bright light will maintain its purple color. Warmth and high humidity are preferred. Waffle plant is subject to browning leaf edges if it is allowed to dry out too often, or if insufficient humidity is provided. The waffle plant belongs to the *Acanthaceae* family.

Homalocladium platycladium

The tapeworm plant is grown more for its unusual appearance than for beauty, and it certainly is different! This plant likes bright to medium light and evenly moist soil. Its natural habitat is the Solomon Islands. The tapeworm plant belongs to the *Polygonaceae* family.

Hypocyrta strigillosa

The goldfish plant from Brazil is really quite beautiful. Its dark green foliage is a lovely foil for the copper colored flowers it produces. The flowers really do resemble goldfish. It prefers bright light, evenly moist soil, and high humidity. *Hypocyrta* is a *Gesneriad*.

Japanese sweet flag: see *Acorus*

Joseph's coat: see *Alternanthera*

Kennilworth Ivy: see *Cymbalaria*

Lamium galeobdolon

A rapid growing creeper, cobra plant is found in Quebec and in Central and Eastern Europe. It is really a very hardy plant and will quickly fill a pot. Cobra plant prefers a bright to medium light and evenly moist soil. It's a thirsty plant like the waffle leaf. A cool temperature is preferred. Propagate from stem cuttings. The cobra plant belongs to the *Lamium* family. (It's a relative of the *coleus.*)

Lipstick plant: see *Aeschynanthus*

Lotus berthelotii

The parrot's beak is so named because of the scarlet flowers it produces. Its natural habitat is the Canary Islands and Cape Verde. It likes a bright light and evenly moist soil. The *Lotus* belongs to the *Leguminosae* family.

Lysimachia nummularia

Moneywort or creeping jenny is a charming trailing plant, a little bit on the difficult side to grow. It likes evenly moist soil, but the paper-thin foliage is easily rotted if you water directly onto it. It likes a medium light and enjoys being misted. Keep it pinched to stimulate branching and discourage lower leaf drop. Propagate from cuttings. This belongs to the *Primulaceae* family.

Mexican flame vine: see *Senecio*

Mikania apifolia

The hanging velvet vine is similar in care and appearance to *Gynura,* or purple velvet plant, except that *Mikania*'s leaves are much smaller and shaped a bit differently. It prefers a bright light and evenly moist soil. It's a very easy plant to grow, but keep an eye out for hungry aphids. The hanging velvet vine belongs to the *Compositae* family.

Ming tree: see *Polyscias*

Mirror plant: see *Coprosma*

Moneywort: see *Lysimachia*

Monkey plant: see *Ruellia*

Nandina domestica

This bamboo from China and Japan is an attractive bushy plant. It may grow up to 8 feet tall, but is usually sold as a much smaller plant. The bamboo likes an evenly moist soil and bright to medium light. Propagate by dividing. *Nandina* belongs to the *Berberidaecae* family.

Nothopanax arboreus

This plant from New Zealand rather resembles the *Schefflera*. It is often referred to as five fingers. *Nothopanax* is sometimes found in the outdoor section of the nursery, but is excellent as a house plant. It prefers a bright light and evenly moist soil. Propagate from stem cuttings. *Nothopanax* belongs to the *Araliaceae* family.

Ornamental pepper: see *Capsicum*

138

Osmanthus heterophyllus

The false holly's foliage really does resemble the true holly except that its leaves are generally smaller. A variegated form has green leaves edged with white. Although often grown outdoors, the false holly is easy to cultivate in the house; all it requires is a bright light and soil that is kept evenly moist. Propagate from stem cuttings or by air layering. Plants whose growth has gotten out of control should be pruned in early spring. *Osmanthus* is a member of the plant family *Oleaceae.*

Oxalis hedysaroides rubra

The fire fern, a pretty plant from South America, has red leaves and produces yellow flowers. It prefers a bright light and barely but evenly moist soil during its growing season. When it becomes dormant, let the soil dry out moderately between waterings. Propagate by dividing. *Oxalis* belongs to the *Oxalidaceae* family.

Paradise plant: see *Strobilanthes*

Parlor ivy: see *Senecio*

Parrot's beak: see *Lotus*

Pellionia

The two most commonly seen varieties of the smoke plant are *P. daveauana* and *P. pulchra*. This creeping plant is extremely hardy and will tolerate low light although it prefers a brighter light. Keep its soil evenly moist and propagate from stem cuttings. *P. daveauana* is from South Vietnam, Malaysia, and Burma, and differs from the other variety in that its leaves are not netted in the center with the blackish vines. *P. pulchra* is from Vietnam. Smoke plant belongs to the plant family *Urticaceae.*

Peristrophe augustifolia

The bright and pretty tiger plant is from Java. It's a rapid grower that will trail if allowed to grow long stems. Periodically pinch out new growth tips to keep the plant from becoming leggy. Tiger plant needs a bright light to maintain its distinctive markings. It will revert to all-green foliage if insufficient light is provided. Keep its soil evenly moist. Propagate from stem cuttings. It is a member of the *Acanthaceae* family.

Plectranthus

There are many other varieties of this genus besides the commonly known swedish ivy. The bushy mint *Plectranthus* may not be much to look at but its soft, fuzzy leaves which are scented like mint are sufficient attraction. The rosy *Plectranthus* has leaves with purple undersides, and it makes a lovely hanging plant. *Plectranthus* species like to be kept evenly moist and in a bright to medium light. They belong to the *Labiatae* family.

Podocarpus macrophyllus Maki

The Chinese podocarpus's natural habitat is China and Japan. It's a very pretty evergreen tree that will stay relatively small for indoor use. Prune to control its shape and size in early spring. The podocarpus likes a bright light, barely moist soil and cool temperatures. It belongs to the *Podocarpaceae* family. Propagate from stem cuttings.

Polyscias

Two popular varieties of *Polyscias* are the ming tree, *P. fruticosa elegans,* and the Balfour aralia, *P. balfouriana marginata.* The elegant ming tree is from Polynesia. It may grow to about 4 feet in height. The Balfour aralia is from New Caledonia. It differs considerably in appearance from the ming with its rounded green leaves edged in white. These aralias are relatively easy to care for; they like bright light, evenly moist soil and a high level of humidity. *Polyscias* belongs to the *Araliacea* family.

145

Pseudoanthermum atropurpureum tricolor

This unusual and pretty plant is from Polynesia. It is rather easy to grow; all it requires is medium to bright light and evenly moist soil. It would also appreciate extra humidity. Pinch periodically to maintain a bushy appearance. Propagate from cuttings. This plant is a member of the *Acanthaceae* family.

Pussy ears: see *Cyanotis*

Ruellia makoyana

The monkey plant is charming, not only because of its unusual coloring—dark green leaves with a red tint and silver veins—but because of the fuzzy texture of its foliage. The red flowers it sometimes produces are incidental. Monkey plant likes a bright to medium light and evenly moist soil. Keep it pinched to encourage bushiness. Propagate from stem cuttings. The monkey plant belongs to the *Acanthaceae* family.

Saint Augustine grass: see *Stenotaphrum*

Sanchezia nobilis glaucophylla

This pretty plant from Ecuador bears a strong resemblance to its cousin, the *Aphelandra* or Zebra plant. Not only are the leaves similar in appearance, but it also bears a yellow flower. The *Sanchezia* likes evenly moist soil, bright to medium light and high humidity. Keep this plant pinched to maintain a bushy appearance. The *Sanchezia* belongs to the *Acanthaceae* family.

Sarcolocca ruscifolia

The sweet box is native to West China. It likes a bright light and soil that is allowed to dry out slightly between waterings. It produces pleasingly scented white flowers. *Scarcolocca* is a member of the *Buxaceae* family.

Sarracenia purpurea

The sweet pitcher plant is found growing naturally from the Carolinas to Labrador. It's a carnivorous plant that grows in swamps. It likes a bright light and wet soil, and it prefers a cool temperature. Add chopped sphagnum moss to commercial potting mixes for better water retention. The pitcher plant is sometimes marked with red, and it produces purple flowers. Feed it flies twice a week for best growth; however, it will survive without a diet of insects. It is a member of the *Sarraceniaceae* family.

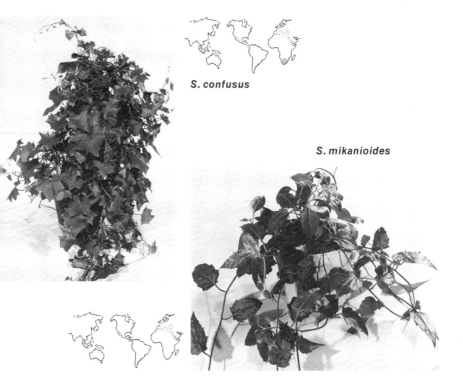

S. confusus

S. mikanioides

Senecio

This plant is available in a vast variety of forms; it may have fleshy, succulent "leaves" or delicate, paper-thin leaves, depending on the variety. Two of the more delicate looking varieties are *S. confusus,* the Mexican flame vine, and *S. mikanioides,* parlor or German ivy. The flame vine produces orange-red flowers, and the German ivy develops yellow flowers, but blooms rather less frequently than its cousin. These plants, especially the German ivy, thrive in constantly moist soil. You may have to water almost every day to keep them from shriveling. They like a medium light and can be propagated from stem cuttings. *Senecio* belongs to the *Compositae* family.

Shrimp plant: see *Beloperone*

Silk oak: see *Grevillea*

Sinningia

The many varieties of the tuberous *Sinningia* are related to the African violet, and like that plant, produce lovely flowers. Probably the varieties you are most familiar with are the spectacular gloxinias. However, the *Sinningia* also comes in a miniature form, with some plants not much larger than a quarter. This plant needs a bright light and evenly moist soil. Because the plant is a tuber (like a bulb) the foliage will die back. After flowers fade, cut back all foliage and flowers to rejuvenate the plant and encourage new growth and more flowers. You may do this several times before it stops blooming altogether. When this happens, cut it back again and store the tuber, still in the soil and pot, in a cool, dim place and water it less frequently until growth begins again in the spring. Propagate from leaf or stem cuttings. The *Sinningia* is a *Gesneriad.*

Smoke plant: see *Pellionia*

Stenotaphrum secundatum variegatum

The foliage of the Saint Augustine Grass reminds me of the spider plant because it is composed of strap-like leaves with color bands of green and white. It likes a bright light and soil that is kept quite moist. Propagate by dividing. This plant belongs to the *Gramineae* family.

Streptocarpus saxorum

This pretty little plant from Tanganyika is lovely not only because of its soft fuzzy foliage, but because it produces white and lavender tubular flowers. *Streptocarpus* is related to the African violet and should be treated in a similar manner. Keep its soil evenly moist, but avoid splashing water on the leaves. This plant requires a bright light and high humidity. Propagate from stem cuttings. *Streptocarpus* belongs to the *Gesneriaceae* family.

Strobilanthes exotica

The paradise plant is striking because of the metallic purple color of its foliage. Its natural habitat is New Guinea. Paradise plant prefers a bright light, evenly moist soil and high humidity. Propagate from stem cuttings. The paradise plant is a member of the *Acanthaceae* family.

Sundew: see *Drosera*

Sweet Box: see *Sarolocca*

Sweet Pitcher Plant: see *Sarracenia*

LIGHT REQUIRED
(*asterisk indicates optimum light condition)

Low	Medium	Good	Bright	Full Sun
		Abutilion	Abutilion	Abutilion*
Acorus	Acorus	Acorus	Acorus*	
	Aeschynanthus	Aeschynanthus	Aeschynanthus*	
Alsophila	Alsophila	Alsophila*		
	Alternanthera	Alternanthera	Alternanthera*	
	Anthurium	Anthurium	Anthurium*	
	Asparagus	Asparagus	Asparagus*	
		Beaucarnea	Beaucarnea	Beaucarnea*
		Beloperone	Beloperone	Beloperone*
	Bromeliads	Bromeliads	Bromeliads*	
			Cacti	Cacti
		Capsicum	Capsicum	Capsicum*
	Chamaerops	Chamaerops	Chamaerops*	
	Chrysalidocarpus	Chrysalidocarpus	Chrysalidocarpus*	
Cissus	Cissus	Cissus	Cissus*	
		Clerodendrum	Clerodendrum*	
	Coffea	Coffea	Coffea	
	Coprosma	Coprosma	Coprosma*	
		Cyanotis	Cyanotis	Cyanotis*
	Cymbalaria	Cymbalaria*		
	Cyperus	Cyperus	Cyperus*	
Darlingtonia*				
Dipladenia	Dipladenia	Dipladenia	Dipladenia	Dipladenia*

1	2	3	4	5	6
		Euonymus	Euonymus	Euonymus	
	Glecoma	Glecoma	Glecoma	Glecoma*	
			Grevillea	Grevillea	Grevi lea*
Hemigraphis	Hemigraphis	Hemigraphis	Hemigraphis	Hemigraphis*	
Homalocladium	Homalocladium	Homalocladium	Homalocladium	Homalocladium*	
	Hypocyrta	Hypocyrta	Hypocyrta	Hypocyrta*	
			Ixora	Ixora	Ixora*
	Lamium	Lamium	Lamium	Lamium*	
			Lotus	Lotus*	
	Lysimachia	Lysimachia	Lysimachia*		
	Mikania	Mikania	Mikania	Mikania*	
	Nandina	Nandina	Nandina	Nandina*	
	Nothopanax	Nothopanax	Nothopanax	Nothopanax*	
			Osmanthus	Osmanthus	Osmanthus*
			Oxalis	Oxalis	Oxalis*
Pellionia	Pellionia	Pellionia	Pellionia	Pellionia*	
		Peristrophe	Peristrophe	Peristrophe*	
	Plectranthus	Plectranthus	Plectranthus	Plectranthus*	
		Podocarpus	Podocarpus	Podocarpus	Podccarpus*
	Polyscias	Polyscias	Polyscias	Polyscias*	
	Pseudoanthermum	Pseudoanthermum	Pseudoanthermum	Pseudoanthermum*	
	Ruellia	Ruellia	Ruellia	Ruellia*	
	Sanchezia	Sanchezia	Sanchezia	Sanchezia*	
	Sancolocca	Sancolocca	Sancolocca	Sancolocca*	
		Sarracenia	Sarracenia	Sarracenia*	
	Senecio	Senecio*	Senecio*		
	Sinningia	Sinningia	Sinningia	Sinningia*	
	Stenotaphrum	Stenotaphrum	Stenotaphrum	Stenotaphrum*	
		Streptocarpus	Streptocarpus	Streptocarpus*	
		Strobilanthes	Strobilanthes	Strobilanthes*	

DEGREE OF DIFFICULTY

Easy

Acorus	Chamaerops	Hemigraphis	Pellionia
Alsophila	Chrysalidocarpus	Homalocladium	Peristrophe
Asparagus	Cissus	Lamium	Plectranthus
Beaucarnea	Coprosma	Mikania	Podocarpus
Bromeliads	Cyperus	Nandina	Ruellia
Cacti	Euonymus	Nothopanax	Sarcolocca
Capsicum	Grevillea	Osmanthus	Stenotaphrum

Moderately Easy

Abutilion	Cymbalaria	Lotus	Sanchezia
Aeschynanthus	Cyperus	Lysimachia	Streptocarpus
Alternanthera	Dipladenia	Oxalis	Strobilanthes
Beloperone	Hypocyrta	Polyscias	
Cyanotis	Ixora	Pseudoanthermum	

Difficult

Anthurium	Darlingtonia	Sarracenia
Coffea	Drosera	Senecio
Clerodendrum	Glecoma	Sinningia

Editing: Terri Bates
Art Direction: John Tullis
Design and Production: Sally Riggs
Illustration: John Tullis
Photography: Tom Symons, Mike Anderson
Typography: Alphabet Express
Lithography: Independent Printing Co.

LIGHT EXPOSURE GUIDE

NORTH EXPOSURE

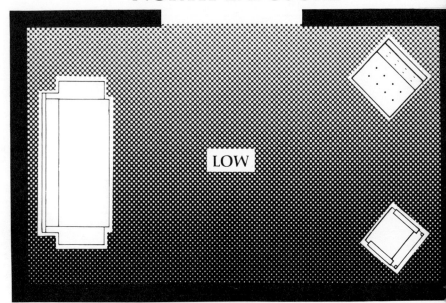

LOW

WEST EXPOSURE

BRIGHT   GOOD